MW01698673

The publisher told you that Wendell Roland Snark was a pseudonym. That is a lie. Wendell was born to Roland and Merry Snark in Pathway New Zealand in 1935. He has a twin sister, Wendella Merry Snark. She was a famous erotic dancer until arthritis of the colon ended her career. Merry Snark has knitted thousands of tea cosies. She was knitting a tea cosy when she died. Merry fainted and fell on her knitting needle and bled to death on their front porch. Roland ran a chicken farm his whole life. He hated sheep. Roland chocked to death on an organic chicken bone. Wendell never married, but fathered three illegitimate children named: How, What, and Why. Naturally, he became a successful head librarian in Pathway. His lifelong companion was transgender. She even hiked in high heels. Even though Wendell is afraid of water, as a child he nearly drowned in a puddle, he has published a series of successful submarine novels. The latest is titled *Dry Doc* where the physician on board struggles to remain sober. Wendell drinks only the local beer. His urine smells of sweet hops.

Dedicated to the gods of human folly.

Wendell R. Snark

On the Eighth Day

Austin Macauley Publishers™
London • Cambridge • New York • Sharjah

All of the events in this memoir are true to the best of author's memory. The views expressed in this memoir are solely those of the author.

A CIP catalogue record for this title is available from the British Library.

ISBN 9781528951609 (Paperback)
ISBN 9781528973175 (ePub e-book)

www.austinmacauley.com

First Published 2022
Austin Macauley Publishers Ltd®
1 Canada Square
Canary Wharf
London
E14 5AA

Foreword: A Crescendo

JoyLand opened on Easter Sunday and closed on Labor Day. When it was alive, it glowed with a dazzling array of painted colors. It had a preposterously frightening roller coaster, a Ferris wheel that swung you to heaven and around you went creating a rhythm of every person's life. JoyLand. Then one Easter JoyLand didn't open. It went bankrupt. And everything went to rot. JoyLand was a morgue for dead clowns. The clowns didn't even keep their outfits. And all the colors faded into oblivion.

It took a year for Parkinson's to wear down my brothers enchantment with life (now a machine that whirls and jerks and tumbles you) It began with a forgetting of words and confusion of time. He couldn't explain his thoughts. And he fell like a prisoner into chasms of dead phantoms. It was the hallucinations that punished him for a life of involvements. When dusk became night, the demons would fly from the FUN HOUSE. Shards of jagged glass silver on one side, a memory on the other side. There was no forgiveness Night was cut in shreds.

I continue to wander and seek a "The End". Some telltale rendering that explains a life of comings and goings. Is this it? Well, dear Wendell, I hope so. *To be read at the gates of heaven.*

Table of Contents

“God created humour
because of all his blunders committed on the
previous seven days.”

Recollections of an old college English teacher.

One

Noise! You probably couldn't tell the difference between the biology students exiting classroom 210 Sentinel and the first-year English students entering. Just a conglomeration of humanity. Clay not yet formed into (real) people – not the broken images of mom and dad. Confusion has its merits. At the break in the first English class of a past semester, two students asked me if this class was biology one ten. In a first class, I never mentioned 'Moby Dick' again.

More noise! In the midst of all the shuffling and banging and thumping, I set my lecture notes on the podium. You can't hear the thumbing through the pages. A student appears. A large one. "Excuse me, sir, are you going to say anything important today? Try outs for the wrestling team start at three."

A large one. "Let me check." I began to finger through the pages of notes. I would flip a page, scrutinize it, and say "No, nothing here." Closing the file folder, I said, "Nope, not a thing with any meaning."

Thanking me for not saying anything important, the large one disappears in the crowd of coming and going students.

I suppose I was right after all. In the rush of western civilization, what I did that day or any day for that matter, would not change its course. English 110 Section C was relatively insignificant. No relativity about it.

Two

Thank God, no bells. Although, there is a clock in the back of the classroom to remind you of how temporary life is. There was a clock. The faculty association got rid of them. Too many students would too often turn around to check on their imminent freedom. 'Time', to me, was a cheap pocket watch I bought at the Vancouver airport. As a matter of fact, it died for good on my very last class. But that is a long way off. Long. Way. Off.

She was standing in front of the podium. Shy. The class was finally over (finally) and the good bye noise was loud. Shy. Very. "What can I do for you?" I heard myself saying. Shy said: "I wonder if you would give me the name of your plastic surgeon. He did a great job." And you wonder why I taught for thirty-eight earth years.

But things must stop here right now. One thing they do not teach you in graduate school or in education departments… the really good stuff… there is no end to the boring crap… you are a public figure that generates endless stories like electrons around an atom's nucleus.

Luckily, you hear only ten percent of the clandestine chatter, but that is really ten percent too much. Way too much. Unnerving much. One story that would circulate every few years was all about my three years working for the CIA. I liked that James Bond story because it was partly true. Well, the partly that includes a desk with an in-box but no pussy galore and no Goldfinger. I actually worked at the National Security Agency, a partner of the CIA. 'Actually' my life is much more interesting in story form than in reality.

Shy said she heard that I was in a horrific automobile accident that wrecked my face. She was quite sad that it wasn't true. Me too. Shy's brother was thrown from a horse and dragged to the corral gate. All I had on me was my allergy medicine and a plastic box of tic tacs.

Three

Mature students are a god send. Really mature students are a miracle. I have had in class seniors in their late eighties. One mature lady would come to class with her book bag and a crocheted pillow (haemorrhoids). These seniors became the class surrogate grandma and grandpa. With enough of them, you could shut down the counselling office.

Next to the campus was an extended care hospital, Mount Saint Francis. The patio with its very own fountain, no coins, had a spectacular view of the lake and glacier mountains. The icy peaks itching the fanatic skiers. On warm spring days, I would hold grammar class on the patio. Inmates, or patients if you prefer, would often sit on the outskirts of class. One old geezer – and why not – leaps up to provide a lecture in a lecture. He yelled at the students to listen to this man (Me, a dumfounded me) and goddamnit, use the semi-colon like he says. I wish I had that old geezer in every class.

The mature students knew the secrets in their life and knew that you learned by confronting those secrets. One mature student had quite a hefty secret. It got him arrested in my class. You maintain interest by having a student arrested in each class. He was balding. His face sagged with wrinkles. He had a pot belly full of lushly rich enjoyments. He had sweet eyes. His voice was soft and scintillating. After every class, he would stop at the desk to wish me well and compliment me on the lecture.

Something was wrong!

Teachers aren't complimented. Brown nosers excluded. The best we can wish for is not to be shot by a bored student and/or angry parents. Father Zwiney S.J. once told me, well, more than once, because he was slightly senile, that in any class one-third will love you, one-third will hate you, and one-third won't give a damn. True, I swear. Although everyone hated Herman Melville.

Something was really wrong!

He never turned in any work. So, when the cops arrested our pot bellied, balding, wrinkled face gentleman, they were arresting the notorious 'Great Canadian Imposter'. For many years, he posed as a psychiatrist. Not that difficult. All you need is a vest, a beard, and a pipe. His clients loved him. Supposedly while posing as a surgeon, he successfully removed an appendix. The faculty loved him too, including their healthy appendices. We wrote a letter seeking clemency. A complement to a teacher is as rare as finding the holy grail in the back of your closet. The law of saying nice things convincingly is a rare and powerful gift. Life being so bleak!

Four

Don't 'ever' stare at the stars. It will make you sick – or at least apprehensive because, you have become suddenly aware of the chaos above your head and even more aware of the calamity beneath your feet. Rivers flowing old land into the sea and volcanoes blasting new earth in rivers of lava. And what do us puny mortals have to explain this inexplicable existence hurrying by our time? A hurrying that is a once and once only happenstance… religion… A whole buffet of religions, handy and ready to serve our immortal souls. Each religion has its very own edifice of holy words that strives to explain 'our place' in the obvious oblivion of life. Is there a dinosaur heaven? Who knows? Who cares if our heaven is slightly overcrowded with all the people and starter people who were ever born? Luckily, the seven plus billion of us stuck on this ball are susceptible to hyperbole.

And love is not the answer. It is not even the question. Because no one knows exactly what it is. We know what it does. We know that comedy cannot exist unless at its core is love. Comedy is love, whereas tragedy is fate yelled into the night: God loves you! God forgives you! But does he? How can you be sure? Is sex even love or the very essence of love? All those inexplicable things that happen every day in life. How do you explain them? You don't! That is why 'the unexpected' poses itself as a possible answer to the delusions of comedy. At least the start of a questionable answer.

Scientists call the unexpected 'flux'. We are calling what happens here on earth and everywhere else the unexpected. And whenever it happens, and the unexpected is always happening, we have the chance for comedy. The Bible, at least for Christianity and Judaism, is the greatest work of comedy ever penned by us mortals. God is always there, somewhere. Does comedy happen even when you stop laughing or the joke wasn't funny in the first place? I honestly don't know.

Like the man whose electrocardiogram read strong and healthy twelve minutes before he died in the hospital parking lot of a heart attack. I wonder what he thought as he lay there on the pavement with his car door open and the car keys in his hand. Was his scream indistinguishable with his laughter?

The unexpected is the dilemma of every human soul. And why a course on comedy is more than just a joke told.

That's how I began the course on comedy. The unexpected. Without anyone knowing, I had confiscated from the kids an old book bag and filled it full of discarded books headed for the dump. I quietly set it by the windows. Class was on the third floor of MacGregor Hall. I suddenly stopped the lecture. I had noticed the book bag. "Whose book bag is this?" I am obviously annoyed. No one says anything. I walk over to the book bag. I am even more obviously annoyed. I slide open the window and toss the book bag out the window. Hear the crash below.

The students are stunned. Their faces are glued with amazement. Shock, really. And then a couple start to laugh, then a few more, and then the whole class is laughing. That, my friends, is the unexpected. And that, my friends, is comedy.

Teaching is live theatre. You never know what will happen next. Yes, indeed, you have a lesson plan, but that is just a placebo. Because of all those people posing as students out there.

It was a speech class for business administration students. It was a demonstration speech. It was a pretend business association meeting. It was Todd's turn and he had demonstrated the difference between basketballs. Who knew? It was one student's duty to introduce the speaker and another student to thank the speaker. Enough of all these 'it was'es'. (All the names are invented, since I can't remember them anyway. I'm old, but come to think of it, I had trouble remembering names when I was young.) Timothy continues thanking Todd. "So, Todd, everyone here in the association want to thank you for bringing your balls to class."

It took a few nano seconds and then the UPROAR! Todd was holding his balls under each arm. These he dropped and they dribbled across the front of the room. Someone yelled, "Now, Todd has lost his balls."

Caught between 'got' to laugh but 'can't' laugh. Not allowed. Not supposed to. Impolite. It is the Les Miserables of life. When I mentioned the now occurring incident in my class, the head of maintenance didn't believe me. I must admit peculiar things were always happening in my classes. I am cursed. (Bob: How did she get her finger caught in the chair? Me: Sorry, I forgot to ask. Me again: Are you going to let her drag this chair through life. She'll probably will never marry. And if she does … Will you take Darlene and her chair for your lawfully wedded wife? Hope she doesn't get pregnant. Bob: Stop it. Okay. Okay. I'm coming. But if this is one of your pranks, you'll get more than a finger.) Oh, good God!

Pandemonium! I mean pandemonium everywhere. Half the class, mostly girls, had nested around Darlene consoling her, while the other half, mostly guys, were in the hall stifling howls. "Well, you have nine other fingers, didn't help." She was so embarrassed. Darlene decided to wait till the end of class and have her boyfriend call her father, a plumber. How we hide our misery from the ugly scrutiny of a savage society! But when she didn't get up at the break and had this wide-eyed look of someone who had to pee and there was no toilet within ten miles, hilarity ensued.

This was a class on Renaissance literature. And in the text, next, was a reproduction of Michelangelo's Sistine Chapel moment when a beefy God reaches down with his finger to touch a steroid plump Adam. I didn't quite make it to the hall before exploding. Sorry! (It took a while, Vaseline and a number seven screwdriver, to free the lovely damsel in distress who could once again finger her life.)

Oh, the shame of it all. MISTAKES! When you wish you were Charlie Chaplin's little tramp and be able to sashay down that lonely road into a narrowing black circle of oblivion. I was describing how the jet ascended Fort Lauderdale International Airport. Banked left. Then proceeded up the Florida coast to Orlando, Chicago, and eventually Winnipeg. Our heroine had met him on a cruise. A rich. Very handsome. Very Mexican. Very, very. They had fallen in love. Madly in love. At Easter, the families were to meet in Winnipeg to plan the nuptials. She held in her hand a love letter from our very him to be opened when the jet reached cruising altitude. When she finally opened the letter, it contained five words. 'Welcome To the Aids Club'. But I was still describing. Below the jet, you could see the famous Galt Ocean Mile where there was one giant condom complex after another. Oh, the shame of it all.

Orange hot coals blazed blue flames. Me, destined for the fires of hell having ruined some of the great classics. How about Herman Melville's 'Moby Dick'? ISHMAEL written on the board in large letters with arrows shooting from his name. Why? Hell, I don't know. ISHMAEL, sole survivor of the Pequod. Alone. Alone in the vast pacific. Without a breeze the ocean mirrored a cloudless sky. Lost in a gray nothingness. ISHMAEL ignored by the gods, doomed by the fates, would go mad. The first existentialist. To emphasize his tragedy, I pounded the black board with my fist. ISHMAEL Why? Hell, I don't know. The BANG caused both my hard contacts to slide off my retinas. Dizzy. Vague shapes everywhere. I staggered a bit. I couldn't see who it was, but someone yelled "It's OK, he's just having another vision."

If ISHMAEL didn't destine me to a hot eternity, then this damned if you do damned if you don't question would. To prepare students for the interview that usually contained a damned question, I invented my own damned questions. This particular one usually enraged bible tooting evangelical fanatics. No unusually about it. You enter the outhouse and shit. You look around for something to wipe your ass. All you see on a tiny shelf is the bible. Do you use the old or New Testament? Why? Hell, I don't know!

WARNING! I have decided on a sex change operation, but I don't know what kind. Please do not ask that sentence why it is funny or not so funny. You may find yourself swimming in the guck of a philosophic stew.

Five

WHAT! What note! "Nothing is working out. Its useless," said with chocking panic. That's Sally, his wife. "Ed took his revolver. He is somewhere out in the woods." This is me, a frantic English teacher. "Call the RCMP. And don't worry. Is that the revolver he built in his father's metallurgy shop? (YESYES) Don't worry. It probably doesn't work anyway." Me, Sally, an RCMP officer are standing on the front stoop of their mobile home. Out of the woods stumbles Ed (YESYES) the useless one, holding in one hand the handle of his revolver and in the other hand – the barrel. It fell off when he pulled the trigger.

In those days, (I almost wrote bygone), there was little help for a dyslexic and lots of misunderstanding. Ed left university with mostly failing grades and a gentleman 'C-' in English Composition. We live along a highway in a Mediterranean style cottage on the side of Elephant Mountain. Yes, it's steep, even for deer and bears. Actually, the cottage is situated on the rump of Elephant Mountain. And during spring runoff, when the water turns brown, you wonder sometimes. I am busy with this rock wall when I notice a logging truck has pulled into our drive. And walking up the hill is Ed. No revolver in sight. This is just one of four of his company's trucks. Sometimes life corrects itself.

But what if the revolver is in your head, what would the mind do then? Easy to pull that trigger. If I had known in graduate school all the funerals I would attend as a teacher, I might have changed my major. There is nothing more wrenching than the death of a young person. The parents are forced to live their child's imaginary life. Their grief never quits. Nor the absurdity of their lost. Nothing is to be found to alleviate their barbed sorrow. Because. Each life is a story book. And the many pages of an old life with its final 'Finis' chapter is a testament as powerful as the other Biblical two. The many blank white pages of a young person's life are screaming at me.

On that sunny autumn afternoon, I didn't hear that plaintive scream as I rushed past some of my students laughing, shouting, teasing, yakking and shoving each other out in front of MacGregor Hall. There he stood. Separate from everyone else. Like a statue in a grotto. Beautiful. The wind did not touch a single strand of his quaffed hair. Complete whereas his classmates were still under construction. Maybe that was why he emitted a strange aura of serene quiet.

There were other contrasts. One stump of a scrawny kid had these skinny appendages, plenty of acne, and those coke bottle glasses. What a grab bag of humanity. A passing scenario only since I was concerned with the return of their first in-class essay. This was their second class and I knew none of the students. Was that a faint scream, no, just the whistle of a CP freight edging up the valley.

If you teach a subject, you depend on your knowledge, but if you teach students you depend on your intuition. There is no science about education – it's a lonely, ignored art.

I was walking around the classroom handing out papers matching name with face with writer. When there it was next in the stack. I was shocked when I read it last night late. I could hardly believe someone so young could write with such awareness of life's situations. And a polished style to boot. I set the paper aside and felt a twinge of apprehension. He must be protected. Something this beautiful must be protected from the savages, the ravage of days of ennui.

I called out the name as I edged toward the scrawny kid. But the scrawny kid didn't raise his hand. The statue in the grotto raised his hand.

When he stopped by the office, good, I wanted to talk to him. I was worried about him. He sat on an old sagging couch in the rich late afternoon autumn sunlight. He was a golden blur. The window looked out on the biology class small vineyard. Whereas everything was dying around them, the purple grapes were ripe for the harvest. I told him how impressed I was with his talent. But I was also worried, such insight in one so young creates a burden. He must be very, very careful.

I wish I had known then, what I found out later. There had been two previous incidents of depression. Once for six weeks in grade school and then again but for six months in sigh school.

He had left his essay for another class on my desk. The note read: 'What do you think of my interpretation'. Oh, it was a cold, cold February day, when he stopped by. I told him how impressed I was. Could I have the essay as a model. Sure, but he seemed rankled. I didn't know what he wanted. Until later. That

August, he stole his brother's gun from his hunting locker, and in the woods blew his pretty face off.

His mother (for some telltale reason) sent me his suicide note. "I can't bare it any longer. Love." His essay was a call for help. I didn't see it in his words. I didn't hear it in the space between his words. He left me only his scream.

Six

(You can skip this section on puns. They are not on the exam.) Some people actually like Herman Melville, but nobody likes a pun. I do. Because they are childish. A pun defines the spirit of a teacher. If you were to strip away the clothes of a teacher, remove his skin, and then search the pile of bones for his soul, you would find a child. A true teacher has never grown up. And that includes all teachers from kindergarten to graduate school. Teachers believe things can and will change. They believe in a God, Santa Claus, and themselves. A yeoman task. Whereas bureaucratic administrators are mannequins. They never change. They just stare at you with blank eyes. "YOU want to do WHAT?"

I was surprised at how early my daughters expressed their sense of humour. Even boisterous laughter. I wondered how early in their development would a child understand a joke. I chose the famous 'Duck joke'.

A duck waddles into a pharmacy and quacks at the pharmacist, "Do you sell nails?" "No, I'm sorry, this is a drug store." The next day the same duck waddles into the same pharmacy and quacks at the same pharmacist, "Do you sell nails?" "I told you yesterday this is a drug store. We have never sold nails here." The very next day the same duck waddles into the same pharmacy and quacks at – yes, the same pharmacist, "Do you sell nails?" "NOOOOO! Get the heck out of here, you dumb duck!" The duck waddles back, you guessed it, the next day. The duck asks the pharmacist, "Do you sell grapes?" "No, we do not sell grapes." "Then, do you sell nails?"

Teachers are not pseudo parents, if anything, they are the lawyer for the defendant – the child. In the joke, the pharmacist represents the parents, who are constantly being annoyed by their brood. The duck represents the child who is stubborn and refuses to learn. I guess you notice the frustration of the teacher.

I began asking the duck joke in college classes and worked my way down to grade two where the kids were more interested in finding out 'stuff' about the duck. Why did the duck want nails? They missed the joke completely. But I was shocked at how thoroughly those third graders 'got' the joke. Frightening, actually. The teacher is a child just to survive the rigors of the classroom.

In my crazy Chautauqua life, I have created single handily two puns. I can die now; my soul is at rest. I sat on the Scholarship Committee. A student by the name of Jacque Dupre (A funny little thing appears above the 'e'. I don't speak French. I don't want to encourage them.) petitioned the committee for some loot. I said I have heard of a jock strap but not a strapped Jacque.

When I entered the classroom, I saw Jimmy Wong and Sally Wong from Hong Kong frustrated, struggling to get their fountain pen liquid cartridge to fit into the pen. (Bic hadn't been invented yet. We actually survived with ink.) I said I see two Wongs can't make it write. They stared at me in utter disbelief. Suddenly, they were transformed into two stark staring bureaucrats. Bic arrived none too soon.

Seven

When it happened, (a premonition) I was walking up the hill to Masden Hall for lunch in the faculty lounge with Father Hansen and Father Doyle (maybe). I am walking… (maybe) I will walk… (maybe) I had walked… (maybe) I had been walking.

Well, which one is it! All of them, probably, none of them, really. I don't know. No one does. Except that time is the theatre in which we play out our lives in all its various fictions. Space, well now, space is the circumference of our reality that sometimes paints and at other times taints our sprit. Although usually quiescent – on occasion it can burst forth in an angry physical orgy. Continents move incredibly slow. Time's clocks have imprisoned us in a simple ticking formula of 'past', 'present', and 'future'. Fabrications. Convenient, yet fabricated.

The outback aborigines exist only in the present. Nothing before, nothing after. No Gods. No Garden of Eden. No mythology. A nothing of nos. Just a now endlessly happening on a nondescript space. Jesus was crucified today… Columbus discovered America today… Einstein published his theory of relativity today. Not at the same time, but in 'no' time. These natives who wrap themselves in illusion may be the original existentialists (move over ISHMAEL).

Some minds, like Joyce and Proust and Faulkner, understood the majestic and satiric quality of time. Clocks, clocks everywhere. And sometimes those clocks read 'The past' that sometimes would overwhelm the present reducing it to a puppet repertory and at other times 'the past' overwhelms the unknown of the future as a dans macabre. The past has seen those steps many times before.

I believe once man releases himself from the shackles of the past-present-future concept of existence, the essence of time will reveal the mysteries of the cosmos. And we will be treated as quaint barbarians.

Christopher 'Chip' interrupted my slog up the hill. He would miss my afternoon class. He wanted an early start. It was a long drive to see his family in Seattle. Not many three-day weekends (just this one).

For a split moment I was standing in front of Father Hansen and Father Doyle setting my tray on the table and hanging my jacket on the back of a chair. I heard myself say, "The strangest thing has just happened to me." As Chip jogged toward the dorms, I felt I would never see him again. My body shuddered and I felt chilled. Then, it all passed as if nothing had ever happened. The fathers glanced at one another. It had separately happened to them this morning when talking to Chip. The shudder, the chill. Neither a Hebrew/Greek scholar, neither an Old Testament Biblical expert, neither a neophyte English teach with dubious credentials had any explanation whatsoever for what just happened to them. Some how there had been a rift in the skein of time…

I sat down and unwrapped my sandwich (ham and cheese, no mustard). Father Hansen dropped another sugar cube into his coffee mug. Father Doyle scooped a spoonful of peas and carrots into his mouth. We never did see Chip again. A few blocks from his home he was hit by a moving van who didn't see him. Christopher died on the payment where he was thrown. An asphalt space in a tick of time. [8:23 PDT Saturday October 12 1965]

Eight

The campus went crazy in the summer. The university had few (some) classes, so the university rented out its facilities to various groups. Two groups were roundly despised by just about everybody (except math professor Evelyn Howard who seldom found himself in reality. Wise to an algorithm, janitors were often leading him to his office. He wandered off one day. I hear to Spain. Never to return. The janitors having lost another academic.).

One of the two despised groups was the bagpipe school. School? Yes, school. It was an infestation. They were everywhere puffing their cheeks blowing groans they called music. Not to mention the squeaky shrieks. Pigs in kilts. Those teaches who couldn't flee the campus plotted to hire an assassin to pick the bagpipers off one by one. Easy to find. Just look for a pile of dead birds who committed suicide.

Scottish warriors rushed toward the enemy just to escape the bagpipes! I escaped the present infestation in the courtyard by moving my afternoon appointments to the cafeteria. Bagpipers tramped to the (we don't serve Haggis) cafeteria mainly to piss and puke. Darlene was already waiting to discuss the class assignment: Karl Shapiro's 'Auto Wreck'. James was first though. I was just finishing proof reading James' report when I noticed this creepy guy hovering over Darlene who was obviously annoyed and nervous. Creepy? Thin greased moustache. Vaseline drowned hair, probably dyed black. Oh, yes, tight silver boots at the bottom of tiny little legs. Is that creepy enough for you? Tight-silver-boots-holding-up-tiny-little-legs crept (naturally) away after I yelled at him.

The cafeteria creep was a SHUTOO. A follower of Guru Bywhome Wesshooto. Guru Bywhome called his gathering a 'Brain Drain' Ashram. (I've invented a name to avoid a holy litigation.) For one week of your life and four hundred and thirty-seven dollars and forty-two cents… Why? Don't ask me. Ask the Guru… You can lose the stress in your life by blanking your mind. Guru Wesshotoo's mind is totally blank. No debate there. Besides solemn Guru Wesshotoo's inspirational talks and plenty of zither music (you may want to take up the bagpipes), the weekly followers would meet three times a day for prayer. If it wasn't raining, the followers would spread their blankets on the lawn and lay face down. Every five minutes, a gong would gong and they would twitch. Shake like crazy. In the morning, they would pray for family harmony. In the afternoon, they would pray for world peace. In the evening, they would pray for a prime pump of masturbation. Exploring and exploding your passions frees the brain of stress. When one Shutoo met another Shutoo, they would chant 'May you be fulfilled'. And the passersby would not nod but glance at each other's breasts. More fanatical Shutoos would help direct the glance into a gaze.

After just a few days of Shutoos, the staff, students, faculty (all of us) wanted the bagpipers to drive these holy freaks from the campus to the nearest hell hole. And that would be The Dog and Suds Drive-In at the bottom of University Hill. Shutoos were rude, and besides being rude, they were lewd, and besides being lewd, they were cheap. Penny cheap. You can tell the cafeteria staff were Shutoo disgusted: mashed potatoes were smashed, a ladle of cream corn was dumped, and a grease-soaked pork chop was sloped on the plate. Many wished – no names please – to shove that zither right up Guru Bywhome Wesshooto's tiny little ass. And stop looking at my left breast. Sucker!

Shutooism continues the grand religious tradition of 'Lasciviousness!' Of all the countless examples of 'Lasciv' which one should I choose to tell you? No contest. Of course, it would be Professor Evelyn Howard's math class.

Professor Howard, Ph.D., arrived at the university in disgrace and left in disgrace. Wearing no underwear which was easily detected because his jeans had giant holes in them. Whenever he ambled to the board, girls in class would gasp. For two weeks Professor proved God exists mathematically. The class was held in rapt attention, many contemplating jumping out the window like an old book bag. I think some actually did. Professor Howard was told he couldn't call everyone in town to offer his services to discern their future by examining the tiles in their bathroom. Professor Howard was told it was a requirement to wear your academic gown at convocation, but forgot to mention you should really wear some clothes underneath that gown. LIE! Professor was not a Ph.D. from Harvard. TRUTH! He was a janitor there. LIE! Professor consumed drugs for severe migraines. TRUTH! Professor experimented with LSD in a ribald group of eccentrics lead by Timothy Leary.

Life changed drastically for Evelyn when his mother died. She was rich. Richer rather than very rich. And he was an only child in so many ways. Mommie died in rhyme. She was run over by a train on the plain in Spain while it rained. TRUE – so help me.

I was meandering down the hill from the cafeteria in Masden Hall to my office in MacGregor Hall when I noticed… suspense…all of Professor Howard's math students in Room 100 were staring out the windows. All, except Professor Evelyn Howard who was staring straight ahead babbling about some number plus or minus, completely unaware of what was occurring on the hillside outside his classroom. Two naked female Shutoos were wrestling in the grass fucking like crazy. They were not quite fulfilled but well on the way to mental blankness. Guru Wesshotoo would have been so pleased. I wonder to this day if you can prove sex mathematically (iambic pentameter aside).

Her hand was trembling slightly as she fiddled with her number seven pencil. Darlene was an 'A' student and conscientious, serious too, dreadfully serious. Marine biology was her goal. The poetry text was opened to Karl Shapiro's 'Auto Wreck'' which she kept tapping with her number seven pencil. She was quite nervous. Which I thought was odd. Also odd: she wasn't looking at me. At first, I thought she was having tremors about the Shutoo creep. Understandable. NO, not that fretting. This fretting. "I have tried a couple of times to write about this poem which I know is the assignment, but I just can't. I don't know why. Could I choose another poem?" My reply was instantaneous. "Sure. Whatever poem you want!" Darlene was quite surprised at how easy it was. Am I that doctrinaire? When she left, we were laughing about the Shutoo creep. I didn't think about Darlene and my permissiveness until I received that phone call six weeks later.

I was at home when the phone rang. There were just a few days left for August. A gruff voice. I thought it was the truck driver from Furniture Exchange about the delivery of a lazy boy chair. "This is Sister Mary Serena in Trail." Pause. "Did you teach Darlene Edwards English." I heard myself blurt "Yes! Ma'am!" I was again in eighth grade at Blessed Sacrament school afraid of some Shakespearean detention. You had to memorize Shakespeare. No wonder people hate The Shakes. Why not memorize calculus. "I am her aunt. Her mother wanted me to tell you that Darlene died in an automobile accident last Tuesday afternoon. An old man blinded momentarily by the afternoon sun swerved into Darlene's Lane. They collided head on. Both died where they crashed." She hung up before I could say anything. But there was nothing to say, anyway.

I just sat there staring at the streaks of sunlight, listening to the dull hum of the dial tone, hearing the shouts and laughter of the children and their friends at the beach. It had happened again. I wanted to talk to Father Hansen and Father Doyle, but by then they were gone – gone down their own passage of time. I wondered if Guru Bywhome Wesshooto had a telephone. I picked up the telephone to phone Mrs. Edwards. NO! I decided not to dial information. The phone was replaced on its cradle. I didn't want to know. I wanted to forget/deny/ignore. Was I somehow responsible? No way. Ridiculous. Then I noticed my pocket watch bought in the Vancouver airport was two minutes faster than the clock radio on the mantel. I wondered which one was right.

Nine

There is tragedy, and then there IS Tragedy! From the birth of Adolf Hitler to the death of Hiroshima. What about the fall of a tragedy? The drama department staged ‘Oedipus Rex’. They must have angered the gods because the production turned into a real tragedy.

The set was magnificent. Many giant stone pillars. Rock passageways. And the arch entrance gates to the ancient city of Thebes. Oh, and the backdrop was painted with the rolling hills of Greece. The design stolen from an Air Canada travel poster.

The house lights dim. A hush descends upon the audience. The theatre is dark. One lone spotlight shines upon Oedipus (Eddy McQuire) standing proud (Eddy is six-two) beneath the stone arch of the city gates. Eddy is dressed in the white royal robes of the House of Oedipus. Eddy raises his long muscular arms to the gods, and when he does, Eddy bellows “I Oedipus.” It was then his royal white robes flew open. Sash on floor. Revealing his kingly pecker. Even Freud would have been impressed. Eddy’s sizeable pecker was stuffed beneath a stretched pair of Calvin Klein briefs. Very. Stretched.

Oedipus grabs for the royal white sash. Stumbles. His shoulder knocks over a giant stone pillar. Samson would have been impressed. It is domino time in Thebes! Pillar after Pillar crumble. The arch crashes down just missing the king who is about to vomit. The falling arch misses Eddy who has jumped backwards tumbling the pillars on the opposite side of the stage. The passageway is flattened and covered with the backdrop of the glorious green hills of Greece. Shredded. Even on a sale fare who would want to fly Air Canada to this disaster. Oedipus has single-handedly destroyed his city. Many Greek citizens of Thebes, including quite a few slaves, would blame his giant pecker. Certainly, the director (Marge Applebee) would. The sash lay forlorn upon the stage.

The Greek chorus panics, screaming, as the city of Thebes falls around them. They rush from the stage, down the aisles, out into the lobby, and some even across the parking lot toward the safety of the Dog and Suds Drive-In. Most of them still screaming. Except a Rotary exchange student from Athens who was accustom to Greek earthquakes. The excited audience applauded wildly. If this was the prologue to the play, the climax would be something else. Father Hansen wondered what God the cast had angered. It appears. Zeus.

Academics! I once stood proudly on Mount Olympus with you. The term 'tragedy' is indiscriminately used today. Everything it seems is tragic. From a snapped shoelace to a student submitting a 38-page paper on 'Spain's Tragic Don Quixote', spelling tragedy – 'tradgey'. Spell check would soon end that tradgey. Tragedy must conform to a formula, so tell us academics. Tragedy equals pride, innocence, fate, ideal, error, and finally ruination. Not necessarily in that order.

All life is sad, seldom is it tragic! NO! I don't believe that at all anymore. I believe every human life is tragic because every human life suffers, and struggles, and eventually must die. Unheralded, unheard, but dead all the same. A cliché-ridden obituary awaits the deceased. Rocks and ants and everything else large and small that HE created, dies, too. Everything you built, everything you created dies too. No more pain, but no more days either. You can certainly hear an old crock like me yakking. The instant a sperm punches a hole in an egg, tragedy begins – inevitably. Inevitably, you will find yourself alone in a deserted railway station waiting for a train to nowhere in particular.

Like Conner Pelosi, left leg nervously bouncing up and down, sitting in front of my desk. Conner is clutching his term paper with a big red 'F' splashed on the cover. I must not print so large. The red 'F' term paper is chocked full of spelling mistakes, grammar errors, fanciful facts, plagiarised references. If you are quoting a publisher, it should be real, unlike the Blue and Gold Publishers in Minneapolis. Why Minneapolis? All it has is Saint Paul and really bad winters. Blue/Gold happened to be the colors of the university. Loyalty counts. A rushed job if there ever was one.

Conner yells! "How dare you insult my girl friend?"

Querulous. "How did I insult your girl friend?"

Defiant! "She wrote my paper."

(I suggest you get yourself another girl friend. I didn't say that. Conner is an extra large one – and quite angry. He was on the university wrestling team before he dislocated his shoulder.)

I didn't want anything on me dislocated.

We are one day from Graduation. I am chairman of the Ceremonies Committee. If the term paper is a failure, Conner fails the course and failing my course will prevent him from graduating. The Pelosis are a large Italian family. I need new tires anyway. No more spaghetti and meat balls at Mama Angelina's Tratatoria. I saw The Godfather. I had overnight become that evil English teacher.

The Connor Pelosi tragedy continues. I was adamant. The paper was plagiarised. Impossible to write a term paper in less than forty-eight hours. But I knew of a way to turn this tragedy (Mama's spaghetti is terrific) into a comedy (I couldn't afford new tires).

I knew a freshman student who was a genius at faking essays and term papers. A fake essay would run you thirty bucks; a term paper completed with bibliography would run you fifty dollars. No science student applied. He could mimic any style. You had to be realistic. If you were an 'A' student, he would write you an 'A' essay. If you were a 'C' student, it must be a 'C' paper. No over nights. He programmed mistakes to be convincing enough. This student, who shall be known by his prison number S3526724, stopped by my office to give me copies of the four essays he faked. I should have been furious. I chose unique assignments to prevent essay purchase on the internet or the clandestine use of the files of most professors hidden in the Student Union. The battle between teacher and student ensues. Remember the duck demanding nails in a pharmacy? Hong Kong students were always being caught. I was so impressed with S3526724's natural writing ability that I wasn't chagrined. Not very long, anyway. I was sorry to see him leave for Saskatchewan and his plans not to return. I walked Conner Pelosi's lost saviour to the elevator. I appreciated even admired his talent, but then I said, "Be very, very careful, my friend, of your gift or you will end up in prison." A few years later, more than a few, because it was a class reunion he attended. S3526724 had a book of his poems published and spent three years in prison for fraud.

Thanks to an administration who also liked eating at Mama Angelina's Tratatoria, Connor Pelosi graduated with his class. Tradgedy becomes comedy. The diploma he received was blank. When he successfully completed one final course, he would receive an actual legitimate diploma. Connor never did complete another course. Instead, he became a very successful realtor. He even had his blank diploma framed. What a duck, huh! It hung in his office. Still there, I gather. Connor did marry the insulted girlfriend. She became a very popular home economics teach. In all the years that we would on occasion bump into each other, it is a small town, insulted girlfriend never once smiled at me

"Teaching is an occupation caught in a morass of masked moralities where right and wrong shadow one another." Lucifer said that long before the rebellion, but God left it out of the Bible.

Room 302 of MacGregor Hall was my office for a decade, probably more. It was the source of much drama, more than drama, tragedy, after tragedy, after tragedy, especially those few years I shared the office with a Chinese mathematician – Chen Lamb. Chen was very Chinese. Sorry, I don't know how you become very anything, but very Chinese he was. At least from a prairie boy's perspective. He always won Monopoly. How, I don't know? And by the way, never play ping pong with Chen. He was Taiwan's army champion. We became close friends.

Sometimes, in writing this recollection, I can't believe I was ever really young. Was that young 'who' really me? Hard to believe. But believing you are old is not a problem. Ugly realities seldom are.

Now back to the drama and all those tragedies. Students found out that Chen could not stand a girl crying. So soon girls would enter our office, complete with Kleenex, and burst into tears. He would always raise their mark. It was like living in the soap opera 'As the World Turns'. Guys not so lucky. Tears and testosterone, it seems, don't mix. After a bit of arguing, Chen would challenge them to a game of ping pong.

Chen's very wealthy family fled Mao's invasion and escaped to Taiwan with just the stuff on their backs. One treasure, Chen has kept to this very day. There is that word 'Very' again. It was kept in the front closet. He brought it down from the shelf above the winter coats. What was brought down was a carved teak wood ornate box. Inside, nestled in a shiny lavender pillow was a vase. It was white with blue decorations. Chen said it was from the Ming Dynasty. I said, "Good Lord, man, it is over two thousand five hundred years old. Take it out of my hands." Trembling probably. No, really. Two thousand five-hundred-year-old plastic I am comfortable with. Now the fall of that vase would have definitely been tragic. No, excuses about it. Chen put the box back on the shelf. He quietly shuts the closet door.

Before the main featured tragedy, a short subject. Short because it concerns Dameon Comenski. Short he might be, but he was the star of the university hockey team. He was not short on professional prospects either. He was short on my course in public speaking. For this institution, the one term course on public speaking was a requirement for all students. I am sure you are getting the drift – and drift we go. Dameon never showed up for a single class. So, I gave him a zero for his silence. I guess the great Comenski didn't need public speaking. He was still playing hockey! When I checked the records, an eight had been scratched in front of my zero. When I confronted the Department Head, he said he had given Dameon a special public speaking course because of his hockey schedule. In the last game of the season, Dameon Comenski blew out his left knee. It never worked right after that. Dameon Comenski sells shoes in Vancouver.

Teachers have an amazing amount of authority in the classroom, but little real or no power at all. And the sooner the teacher understands that reality the happier he will be. Not really. But no job is perfect, sayeth The Lord. Even God's job and God wrote the book. Satan rebelled and Jesus fiddled with miracles. The loaves and fishes cost a fortune. Changing water into wine ain't cheap. Teachers lose power to two forces. I am not saying parents are devils. I guess I am saying their kind of evil. Parents of course want to protect their children from reality. Teachers are in the business of helping kids grow up. My child is perfect in every way, just like me! We often clash!

But the other force is diabolical. It writes the checks. The administration. The battle with the administration is never ending, especially if you challenge the essential principle of education. Students should not just listen to facts, but should be forced to participate in their thinking. Under my tutelage, the staid classroom became a circus. Some administrators said and even believed this! With my word circus arcade of classroom tricks, I hawked a magic elixir that would cure all academic ills. Ridiculous. If anything, all ideas must be challenged. And folks needed to be tricked into learning. Having fun was a guise that concealed a designated learning objective. I guess I was the Indian people's coyote. Administrators' brains were binged when my classes became very popular. Even some (quite a few actually) colleagues thought I was a charlatan and one female student would now and then come to my office door and yell "Satan!".

Speaking of Satan, if he is in his Hell and God is in his Heaven, then surely on earth there are loopholes a teacher can exploit to gain his freedom. They don't teach loophole-ing in education programs. It is a gift.

Now, after sufficient delay…

The tragedy of Cynthia Tall Grass

Even though it happened years ago, I still remember her revulsion and despair. What I want to forget is her fear and her total sense of helplessness. Poor Nora. Poor Hamlet. Poor Willy Loman. Poor me. Especially poor me. The elders were surprised – no, shocked – when Cynthia Tall Grass petitioned the chief for money to attend university. Rejected without discussion. First of all, she was a girl. There was no second or third reason. Just like her mother, they whispered. Her mother, echoes in the leaves, had a rattle snake tongue. Poisonous! Wherever she walked, the magic pebbles in her pouch would clack. No member of the Nexezem band had ever attended college. The mother and child are flaunting the traditions of the Nexezem people – people of the High Meadow. NO! NEVER! Not until the sun turns black. The chief and his elders in their anger forgot about eclipses.

When the elders discovered that Cynthia Tall Grass had petitioned the Federal Government's Department of Indian Affairs for a scholarship to attend university, they shunned her. When the elders discovered that Cynthia Tall Grass had been granted a four-year scholarship complete with room and board, they banished her from the Nexezem band.

When Cynthia Tall Grass arrived on campus, she was warmly welcomed. She had met (more like seen) very few white people and spoke English only in residential school. Cynthia was dismayed then horrified at her anger. She hated us. Hated us for the fire water, the iron horse, the thunder stick, and for the pale face very existence. Cynthia Tall Grass had forgotten that she had lived with her anger for so long that it had become her very nature. Wherever she went, she isolated herself in a circle of resentment. Cynthia Tall Grass roomed by herself. She drove away any roommate. All of them. She would sit up all night just staring at them. One culture was dying, and the other culture was dead to her. Cynthia Tall Grass was alone.

Cynthia Tall Grass had a reputation of being sullen, even surly. She seldom spoke. She wasn't pretty at all. Her face bloated, scared with acne. And she was slightly chubby. But those jade black eyes could sizzle your ego if tasered at you. Cynthia Tall Grass had the highest academic record of any student.

My face grew paler and paler as I noticed her name on my class list for Literary Criticism 405. Almost all third and fourth year, courses were taught as seminars. An elite and sophisticated educational method. No more than fifteen students and these students were expected to discuss each others' papers. Unfortunately, the system was too expensive, and the university went bankrupt. I knew there would be a Tall Grass problem. Little did I realize just how big a problem. The classroom is a mind field. But since the days of Conner Pelosi, I had become less doctrinaire and more pragmatic. The pragmatism still had a modicum of arrogance. I just wouldn't call on Miss Tall Grass. And I didn't! No Indian war for this brave. Cynthia Tall Grass did not say a single word all semester long. There goes the seminar method. Her term paper was brilliant. It could have been submitted in any graduate school. She received an 'A+'. I was very proud of myself. No arrow in chief yellow feather's ass.

Pull up the leather chaps, I had spoken too soon. My ass was about to be involved in a monumental clash. Little big horn size. Cynthia Tall Grass had deliberately postponed that required course for all students to graduate. Until now. The last semester. Cynthia Tall Grass chose my section of public speaking to deposit her chubby little sealed lips self. Maybe she dreamed, hoped, begged the course requirement would disappear. Like the Nexezem language itself. But note 'public'; in fact, note 'speaking'. Little did I realize that this teach was about to become a dreaded administrator.

It was her turn to speak. Cynthia Tall Grass stood erect behind the podium. Defiant! With those stark black eyes, she stared at her audience. You could have heard a feather fall. Cynthia Tall Grass did not see a classroom of college students also alarmed at public speaking. She saw invaders, white soldiers, trampling on the sacred land of her ancestors.

She threw up.

Vomited all over the podium.

Fled the classroom.

Cynthia Tall Grass would not return. And she left me with a freaked class with wide eyes as if they had seen the end of the world. Any one like to pee their pants next? Which, as a matter of fact, happened years later when I noticed a trickle of urine flowing underneath a desk.

I never asked her to speak again. I would never have her confront her terror again. Actually, anger. She never offered to speak again, although Cynthia did shove under my door all the scripts to the speeches she was obligated to present. What to do, what not! After all the course was called 'public' 'speaking'. (Please don't remember Dameon Comenski)

She must speak. She must say a single word. Grades are due today. Worse. Worse for chief yellow feather's ass. Publicity exploded. First native university graduate from the Nexezem band. A girl! Top of her class! The chief and elders accepted humbly full credit for her stunning accomplishment. They planned to attend the convocation in full regalia. Complete with drums, a powwow, and a tepee or two tepees. Maybe even three. Mama (Echo in the Leaves) was awarded by the proud tribe a new wardrobe – beads and a bunch of new pebbles to clack. Most frightening. The administration was salivating over all the free publicity. TV cameras, microphones, reporters. Hoopla. I don't know how you say it in Nexezem.

And then there was little old me with that little empty box to fill in. The department head would support my decision no matter what it would be. His yellow feathered ass was not available for scalping.

I invited Cynthia Tall Grass to my office and had her sit beside my desk. I spoke very softly to her asking her about her summer plans. She just had to utter one word to pass my 'public' 'speaking' course. I know, I know!

Not a peep. Chen had migrated to the CIBC empire in Toronto, so I had the whole office to myself. I divided the office in half with bookcases. I put couches on one side for small discussion groups. I invited her to sit on one of the couches. I stayed on the opposite side with my desk and files. No confrontation now. I asked her if she wanted a cup of coffee. Not a peep. Although she was breathing. But was that enough to pass her… Please, no more quotation marks… Public speaking. Peep-less.

Then, it happened.

Some medicine man, I would never call him a witch doctor, took pity on me. Cynthia Tall Grass 'sneezed'. Congratulations, you have just passed public speaking one hundred. And printed an 'A' in the once empty tiny box. And why not. She deserved to be the top student. I quickly ushered Cynthia Tall Grass out of my office in case she had a tomahawk hidden in her saddle bags.

At the Convocation Ceremony, Cynthia Tall Grass stood glum with a scowl on her powdered and painted face. Squaw garments adorned her body. Shy!

Overwhelmed! Many spoke for her. She was lost in the pageantry of the moment. Surrounded as it were with the members of her tribe and members of the university tribe all dolled up with their glorified dime store smiles.

In some flush of the moment, her stark black gaze found me, and I suddenly realized Cynthia Tall Grass fully intended to fail that public speaking course. Hypocrites all of you (us)! Whether she intended this revenge or not is mute. The vomit was real. But was it beyond her anger and hatred? I don't know. I never will. But to this very day, I believe she wanted her revenge on all of us.

I wish I had an ending to this story. What happened to Cynthia Tall Grass? But I don't and I won't fake it for a cheap denouement. I did hear she worked a lifetime in the library of the BC Government. I also heard she was working as a cook with a forestry crew in Northern Alberta. No tragic stage, sorry. Comedy, tonight.

Ten

There are many ways to ruin a party besides your girlfriend inviting a talking snake to the Apple Festival. How about a flu epidemic? Those few hardy guests left on the walk to the street splotches of vomit. It was that kind of party. Or how about the party that dragged on until noon the next day because of the massive blizzard. Snow shovelling with migraines. I still squirm with the memory of getting the date wrong for my roommate's surprise birthday party. "SURPRISE!" everyone yelled as my stunned roommate glanced to see who was standing behind him. Sadly, all have happened to me, except the talking snake fiasco.

After this next party debacle, I should be banned from ever throwing another wingding. And if I did who would have the nerve to show up. Probably only zombies!

A beautiful sunny August afternoon.

A good start. It was a beach bash for the summer school students in my Modern Drama class. Sounds fine to me. Our beach has clean white sand. Burgers and dogs cooking on the barbecue grill, beer in the cooler, gin in the watermelon, potato chips and condiments sprawled like strewn puzzle pieces on the picnic table. Oh, yes, a paper plate stacked with freshly baked chocolate chip cookies. Now tell me what could possibly go wrong?

How about an uninvited guest arriving? It was a Modern Drama class after all. At first you couldn't tell the difference between the students splashing and yelling and those students screaming as the corpse floated up on our clean white beach.

It is true that if you stare into the eyes of a dead person, the gaze of the dead person will hypnotize you. Somcone had the nerve to reach down and close his eye lids. The corpse was wearing a dark blue suit and striped tie. Black and gold.

Expensive. His face had a grey pallor to it. Lips slightly bloated. The corpse was quite handsome except of course he was dead.

Six weeks before the beach bash, a red Corvette convertible sports coup flew off the road near our house. It plunged into the lake disappearing between the boulders. His seat belt was not used.

They didn't find the accident until the next morning. RCMP divers could not find a body. Not surprising. There are at least count 129 bodies sunk in the frigid depths of Kootenay Lake mostly fed by glaciers. Sometimes a corpse will bubble with gas and pop up. But not often. 129 not often.

The RCMP came. The coroner came. The ambulance came. The fire chief, for some reason, came. Our very subdued guests left. After, of course, picking up their belongings and picking through their 'we-should-be-going' apologies. We ate hot dogs and hamburgers for weeks. We didn't eat chocolate chip cookies for weeks. The chocolate chip cookies – everyone – were gone, including the plate.

Eleven

Not every small Catholic university in the wild hinterlands of British Columbia would have the distinction of claiming one of its graduates was shot to death in Tehran by an Ayatollah Ruhollah Khomeini firing squad. Usassani Kotzetag!

Usassani Kotzetag's slaying caused a fierce controversy between the university community and the town's citizens. Both wanted to pull the trigger. Ayatollah Ruhollah Khomeini wasn't as despicable as the deceit inside the malignant mind of Usassani where duplicity became an art form. He was huge with shinny lies and skimpy with paying bills. Although Kotzetag never remembered who you were, an anybody, you never forgot Ussasani. Like a snake bite.

I couldn't believe my eyes. There sat Usassani Kotzetag addressing the members of the admissions committee. He – of course – didn't recognize my anybody-ness. Usassani had just handed out to the members of the committee a postcard signed personally by John F. Kennedy. Problem. There were probably 650,000 of these personally signed postcards. I know I passed a handful of them at a Kennedy rally after the first Nixon debate.

My wife worked in the university office one summer. She knew Usassani well. He was constantly in the office getting 'stuff'. Half the women were gooey googly eyed over his swagger, while the other half considered him a shabby gigolo. Watch your purse and your virginity. The scuttlebutt was that Usassani was expelled from Georgetown University because he was caught cheating. Probably.

Usassani explained to the committee that he didn't complete his degree because he had to flee. Sevak, the Shah's secret police, were after him. Probably.

Usassani Kotzetag was a schemer playing all sides and a few middles. One of his duplicitous techniques was to tell 'A' that 'B' said 'A' was an asshole. Then Usassani would tell 'B' that 'A' said 'B' was an asshole. If they were not suspicious, and didn't check with one another, resentment, even bitterness, was secured.

Usassani was a spy for Sevak. I am sure of that. Why then would the other Iranian students on campus hate and fear him so. One dire report and you would be snatched home and your family would be in jeopardy. Iranians love poetry and these whispers were heard early in the morning after the Persian poetry club met. Usassani was anathema to them.

The committee was suspicious. I didn't say anything derogatory. My feet were stuck in the muck of a moral dilemma. The university needed, desperately needed, students. If accepted, wickedness would surely take root. Naiveté, yes, I guess. Certainly idealism. I convinced myself that I should not ruin his chance to change and succeed. Practicality won and wickedness did take root.

When Usassani fled, he owed quite a lot of money to quite a few businessmen. Broke some hearts, in fact, quite a few. Three women showed me a pearl necklace, a family heirloom from the era of the Silk Road, that Usassani had bestowed upon them. He actually bought the necklaces at F. W. Woolworth for $5.96 each. He wrote a check for them that, yes, bounced, and is still bouncing.

Usassani Kotzetag darkest treachery was sowing discontent in the Student Union hoping to convince the students to support the administration in the present campus political turmoil. The administration was controlled by Bishop Fitzgerald – an ardent catholic. The faculty had committed heresy by being secular and international. Bishop Fitzgerald was dismayed that burning heretics at the stake was outlawed at least in Canada anyway. Obviously, compromise would have been a loaf and fish's miracle. The students eventually joined the faculty against the administration. The university, paralyzed by this ideological conflict, would eventually haemorrhage to death.

Usassani's blatant conniving ostracised him among the students. Knowing the administration and Usassani, there just had to be a deal. Somewhere! But what? He did nothing for free, not even pearl family heirloom necklaces.

I ruined my chance to find out. It would be a year or so later when I discovered the deal. Then, I was acting head of the English Department. I thought it was funny when Usassani Kotzetag, the entire kit and caboodle of him, entered my office. This was just after he had been accepted as a student. I should have posed as a confident, but I am not as devious as I thought I was. Before he could song and dance me, I turned to him… I know who you are and what you did… I opened my desk drawer and pulled out my J.F. Kennedy personally autographed postcard. Usassani Kotzetag suddenly became a history major.

Remembering the only time I ever actually talked to Usassani, I just knew there had to have been a 'deal'. It wasn't until Usassani Kotzetag was executed did I find out. The registrar secretly showed me Usassani's official transcript. He had straight 'A's' in Arabic Studies. Problem. The university had no program of Arabic Studies. Also, his 'F' in French, VOILA! was changed to a funny looking 'A'. Instead of an ink eraser, a new foot was added to the 'F'.

The day after convocation Usassani Kotzetag disappeared. Fled. As if the university and the town never existed. For the many who were intoxicated by him, they were suddenly very sober. Ditched wedding plans. Pearl necklaces for sale. The next we heard, rather saw on the CBS evening news, Usassani Kotzetag was standing next to the Ayatollah Khomeini. They were in Paris just before the Ayatollah's triumph return to Iran. The Shah, sick, was dethroned. The two-thousand-year-old monarchy in exile. Disbelief. Our Usassani Kotzetag was appointed the Ayatollah's Foreign Minister.

I am guessing here, but Usassani Kotzetag for the very first time in his entire life wanted to do something right. He wanted peace with the western powers (and naturally kick backs). The Ayatollah was virulently anti western. I gather Usassani's boss, his god, didn't care for Kotzetag's clandestine machinations. Too bad Usassani didn't study more diligently his Arabic Courses.

Today is the day.

So the press has reported. The execution by firing squad of the Iranian Foreign Minister – Usassani Kotzetag.

I don't know the time difference between Tehran and the Kootenays. But as I climbed the last steps to Marsden Hall, I heard a loud boom that echoed down the valley. They were blasting to widen the North Shore Road. But it could be, why not, the fired shots from the other side of the world killing the Foreign Minister. I smiled. I laughed. Good luck, Lucifer. I almost feel sorry for you

Some stories never die. They can last longer than plutonium. That's why it's better to tell the story than be in one. I am sitting on a stool at our island in our new condo. A novel is uselessly open, but I am contemplating the horror of being recently diagnosed with Parkinson's disease. In bounds the manager, Dale Allen, to fix a bathroom plug. He suddenly stops. "Didn't you teach English at the university?" It was forty, well, almost forty years ago. I was surprised he even recognized me.

We were into a tangled switchboard of reminiscences – the do you remembers. Suddenly, our chatter became incisive. It was when Dale talked about his dorm mates – three to a room. One would become a Member of Parliament who would die in a plane crash. Another would be executed by firing squad…

… Wait a minute. What did you just say.? Dale was dazzled by Usassani. He was so courageous to defy the secret police. His life and his family were endangered of being assassinated. The Iranian Embassy in Washington pressured Georgetown University to expel him. Why he is hiding in the Kootenays. He died defending freedom. Dale remembers a postcard Usassani showed him. John F Kennedy had signed it…

Twelve

DIAMOND and HOLLYWOOD or was it HOLLYWOOD and DIAMOND! Who could tell with all that glitter? They stood together blocking the entrance way to my office. That included two gigantic gleaming white grins. I kept looking for the rest of the Mardi Gras parade! I gulped this out loud: "What's with the suits?" They had deep baritone voices. You thought they had swallowed a saxophone. Caterwauling evangelical negro preachers. Hollywood replied: "The man wants to see us!" The man being the registrar who got the university into this mess in the first place. The registrar with his administration buddies were frustrated athletes. Men, no age requirement here, dream of being athletes. Especially book bound bumpkins. Women, on the other hand, just dream about athletes, well, having one. And they don't have to actually be an athlete, just look like one. This of course causes ire amidst the bumpkins' testosterone.

If you knew this fact, wouldn't you be a frustrated administration jock. The university did not have a winning team in any sport as far back as the last ice age. The wrestling team in one weight class won third place, but unfortunately, she tripped stepping off of the podium and broke her collar bone.

So when our registrar's buddy, the registrar of a small college in Topeka, Kansas, mentioned that two of their star basketball players had lost their scholarships due to austerity, our registrar jumped at the chance for that elusive victory and did ten push ups in his office. Two athletic scholarships were quickly awarded from a slush fund like Aladdin's lamp. Rub the rusted old lamp and then rub the genie's ass and out spouts whatever bucks required.

Only one problem – Hollywood and Diamond didn't know how to play basket ball. They sure knew how to argue with the referees though. The university was banned from playing in Spokane, Washington for five years

Hollywood and Diamond or was that Diamond and Hollywood had another problem. Whereas their verbal vocabulary was astronomical, their composition skills were negligible. A sentence was beyond their grasp as I gather so was a free shot. They could not believe I had not accepted them into my first-year English class. Mr. Rogers would not have accepted them in his neighbourhood. Yet! But! Their illiteracy did not stop their verbosity. It enjoined them to new wuthering heights. The verbal artillery that blasted from their mouths was truly wondrous. Chen where are you when I need you?

But I didn't need ping pong. I had a secret weapon. I had studied in Baltimore at John Hopkins. Baltimore was Hollywood and Diamond's hometown. While living in Baltimore, I got to know some Negro Mamas. They are a force unto themselves. I picked up the telephone. Give me your phone numbers. I want to talk to your mamas.

They disappeared!

Only star dust was left behind in my doorway.

Next thing we heard! Our boys, Hollywood and Diamond, were playing basketball in Saskatchewan. Next it was baseball in New Zealand. Only Diamond and Hollywood would dare to argue with the Māori's. And if anyone could convince NASA to permit them into a crew bound for Mars, it would be Hollywood and Diamond.

Thirteen

At the very center of a tragic world is an Incubus – an evil spirit. The Incubus wakes at night and sits on your feet watching you sleep, creating the shadows in your nightmares. Diabolical! At the very center of a comic world is a Sprite, who laughs at the foolishness of silly crazy mortals, creating the pratfalls from the conceits of human pretensions. A prankster!

A successful teacher must avoid becoming the Incubus and endure the wiles of the Sprite. The good teacher must learn to play the fool. He does that by being secure in his humanity. Not afraid of it. Because. His students are essentially babies, babies who will see right through him and around him. And 'Him' cannot escape their laser gaze.

They were born that way. It is their only survival. The minute they are born and for the next eighteen months all they do day in and day out is watch you. Calculating! Don't forget for nine months they have been listening to you. At the end of eighteen months, they know who you are and how to get you. After grasping the nature of a parent, a teacher is an easy mark.

Tensions abound. The classroom is not a quiet place. The teacher knows the world and they don't. And they will resent you for that. You are the enemy of their innocence. So, they mock you as something very, very flabbergasting. "Stop acting like a child!" I can't, that's what I am suppose to be. "Oh, grow up!" Not for a while yet.

And that my friend is 'The 24/42 Rule.' It appears in our story just in the nick of time. You are a baby until your 24th birthday. You are not responsible for your actions. Forgivable for some really dumb decisions. But at 24, you are now responsible for all your actions and pay for all the consequences from those decisions. Quite the birthday cake.

At 42, you begin – just begin – the ordeal of judging your self, your life, your world. You have made many decisions since you were 24. Now you must figure out what has just happened, and inside those happenings, are there any hidden whys? You will become Judge Jury prosecutor defence attorney. And what judgement are you seeking? You may be surprised.

With what I have done and with what was done to me, AM I HAPPY?

After that sweep of time from 24 to 42, you will float like a leaf spun in the currents of a vast dark river that flows eventually into oblivion.

What does all this verbiage mean? A good teacher must always love his students, they're babies, so love them no matter what they do or what they will become. Why? Because of what the world will do to them., what the world has done to you.

Fourteen

OUTRAGEOUS! True, true, true, true, true. What do you do? I gather many have wanted to ask me 'That' question, just because my classes were so different, but they never did ask it to me directly. And it is such a glaringly simple question. (What do you do that they listen so?) Simple questions are the most difficult questions to ask and to answer. I don't remember now which Department Head actually asked me that question. I had quite a few Department Heads over my years teaching.

One was a priest who solved his hair loss with a boot black toupee. When he left the priesthood, I helped him move. I found in his closet two cardboard boxes. One contained Bibles and the other held muscle magazines. That pretty well summed him up. He was a dynamic lecturer. One lecture he gave while standing on his desk. He married quite often, so often I lost count. He broke off the relationship with his gardener and began one with his chauffer. Ever since his ordination he dreamed of a chauffeur driven limousine. (Actually, it would be a Datsun)

One was a divorcee, whose 'ex', a handsome man with dark red hair and shinny brown eyes, hid his homosexuality in their marriage until after the birth of their daughter. She looks just like him. Wild. With those shinny brown eyes. There was one painting that he loved dearly. She kept everything he wanted, especially that painting. One year later, she dumped everything, including that painting. She sent him a picture of the dump. She ate men for breakfast, lunch, and dinner. She died a gruesome death. Liver cancer. She withered away, turning a bile chartreuse. Over the telephone, she still had that edge in her voice. And they say she never lost it.

One was a widower who became so frustrated with the grading system (only the mark counted, not the material) that in a Victorian Literature Class she awarded everyone an 86. There was a celestial blunderbuss. The top students felt cheated, the bottom students felt guilty. Now that's a teacher. Such a sweetheart to allow the fates such turmoil. An English couple was invited to dinner. All through hor'durves and the soup course, he insulted her American citizenship. Finally, she walked to the door, opened it, and said "Get Out!" She dumped their soup bowls in the toilet. She left for Seattle to be with her son… who then moved to San Diego. She committed suicide. Why? Too many strangled relationships. She didn't know what grade to give her life.

One was a dark and foreboding Scottish intellectual who not only earned a doctorate in Medieval Literature but also earned a law degree. He could argue for hours with a judge over a comma. One judge took his cavil and beat himself senseless. He tried everything to get me fired. I was laissez-faire about commas. When the university closed, he opened his own law office. He bilked two estates out of a considerable amount of money. Before being arrested, he took all his commas and fled. Years later he was arrested in Ponca City Oklahoma, sitting in a basement apartment, eating a frozen dinner off a tv tray while watching Jeopardy. He had become an Assistant Librarian at Dwight D. Eisenhower High School. After years of nefarious scheming, (once threatening a sex change operation), he was extradited from the United States. He is serving four years in a maximum prison. The last time I saw him before incarceration he was leaving Wal Mart with his girlfriend, who dyed her hair fire engine red. She was pushing a cart full of toilet paper. I wonder what new scheme was being hatched. Commas beside the point.

I was about to close the classroom door when one of the four stopped by and peeked in. Each student was holding their very own teddy bear chosen from a large box on my desk. We were studying 'The adjective' and 'Obsession'. "How do you do it, you know, get them so involved?" (She) had no idea of fun, so my first answer was nullified. (She) was staring at the large sentence on the front board.

The fox jumps over the dog

"I honestly don't know," I heard myself saying. But that was a lie. My classes are carefully planned and timed under the guise of amusement. Our students were raised in a visual world, so each class was like an episode in a tv series. Hollywood has come to academia. With that sharp edge in that always critical voice, (She) didn't deserve an answer nor would (She) ever truly understand. But you do.

I have my very own Sprite!

My Sprite is notoriously gullible, and by nature easily tempted, usually by other Sprites. I wouldn't say wicked – at least not in front of her. I believe in Sprites. Sprites don't care if you do or you don't believe. They can't be bribed. I know I have tried. Remember Sprites love commotion (and are cowards when things go rye).

And commotion was about to occur in my little life. The Sprites knew I was to invigilate my very first exam – ever. They couldn't resist – just couldn't. Thanks to them an 'Incident' would happen that has never happened to me again. Nor have I heard it happening to anyone else. They're good, those Sprites, very good indeed!

Over the years, and way too many of them too, I have witnessed some remarkable schemes of cheating in exams. The Sprites love them. In fact, I suspect they encourage them. Hide the textbooks and notes in a bathroom stall. Tell the invigilator that you have to pee (urinate if it is a history exam). Don't drop the folded exam, hidden under your sweater, into the toilet. And hope there is no electronic eye. You would not believe how many Sprites encourage janitors to clean the restroom and deposit said books and notes to Lost and Found! Most students have to pee after that. A lot.

If you use ink to print key facts on your wrist, palm or arm, don't sweat. If you write notes on Kleenex and stuff them very carefully back into the box, hope the student with a cold doesn't ask you for a tissue. You heartless asshole. Or hope this invigilator doesn't sneeze while passing your desk and grab a tissue with the history of Greece scrawled over it. Snot and ink smudges all over your crumpled diligent work.

In a large lecture class, if you hire some asshole to take your exam, make sure he doesn't print his own name on the exam booklet.

If by chance exams are held on the third floor of Anderson Hall, usually, sit by the radiator next to a slightly opened window. Create a wire pulley system. Have your room mate in a car right below the slightly opened window. Make absolutely sure that it is not a no parking zone. Send the question down the wire. Textbooks and class notes are in the back seat. Make sure your room mate only smokes nicotine. Send the answers back up the wire. Make sure the slightly opened window doesn't slam shut slashing the wire and snapping your chance to remember that algorithm.

Or how about this one. Attend the examination. Read the exam – if you can. Leave the exam on the desk. Walk out of the exam. Fly free first class non-stop to Hong Kong on Cathy Pacific. The very same airlines that your father owns plenty of common group A stock. As you strut down the grey empty corridor, don't jeer at the Sprites. They just may encourage your English teacher to air mail a copy of the exam to your father (it was never returned).

I have on occasion become an associate member of the Sprites. I was studying in a quiet empty conference room. The door opens. In walks the constitutional law Professor attached to a young student who for some reason (probably fraudulent) missed the mid-term exam. I offered to leave. No, not necessary! So, I didn't leave. Said constitutional law Professor leaves. Footsteps fade down the hallway. The-poor-I-missed-the-exam-probably-fraudulently-student leaves, not before checking the empty hallway for any roaming constitutional law Professors. Quickly returns with books and notes. Spreads them out all around the exam. You wonder if there are any Sprites around.

Yes… there are.

Footsteps in the corridor, growing louder, pausing in front of the door. Muffled sounds of books and notes being scooped up. Deposited on a neighbouring chair and slid under the table. Professor of constitutional law sticks his head in the door. "Just wanted to check if you understood all the questions." (Not until you remove your shitty little head). All is quiet and the books and notes surreptitiously reappear around the exam.

I excuse myself, but deliberately leave behind my black jacket. I walk away toward the elevator. Wait a minute, no, three. Return to the conference room. Listen for the rustle of books. Shoved papers grabbed. "Sorry, forgot my jacket." If anything, Sprites are sincere.

I head for the student lounge. Dramatic strategy was quickly planned for our assault. Elevator door opens. Muffled footsteps growing louder. Footsteps pause at door. Dialogue occurs. Assault one: young excited couple looking for a place to make out. Assault two: violinist looking for a place to practice. Would my playing bother you? Assault three: two students looking for the class on The Theory and Practice of Communism. I thought sure they said this conference room. Assault four: giggling chortling girls talking about who is hot and who is not. Assault five: fierce argument between roommates ending with one being shoved against the conference door. Oh, don't forget the stray walkers just passing by. There was more traffic on that corridor than during the last fire drill.

No one took the course seriously. I didn't have many courses that failed. This was a second-year class: Creative Writing 210. The Sprites couldn't believe their luck. Bullshit one-oh-one. Three free credits. The more astute I got the more ludicrous they thought the whole exercise. I am surprised they even came to class. Too taunt. That's why!

I tried everything to jive the class, to shock their middle-class sensibilities. The world is your classroom! I held classes in the court house, the hospital, the lumber mill, a roadside cafe, but what finally shocked them was to be locked in a jail cell at the local police detachment. I went too far. The line between fiction and reality had been blurred. The clang of the steel door locking them in was too shocking. I had made my point but lost the class.

One other time, I made the same mistake. Just being much too clever. A Sprite news bulletin! It was a Romantics class and the students loved these poets. I privately thought they were sissies. Next to the campus was an extended care facility – Mount Saint Francis. I knew Sister Mary Virginia. The fourth floor was death row. The project was quite simple which should have been a Sprite warning. "All I want you to do is take the stairs to the fourth floor. You will be alone. Then, one at a time, slowly walk down the corridor glancing in at the various rooms. At the end of the corridor, take the stairs down to the garden where I will be waiting for you. I will ask you this question – Did any poem you have studied this term help you understand what you saw on your stroll down the fourth-floor corridor?" It was a mistake, a dreadful mistake. They were shocked and so their thinking stopped. It helped not one iota to understand the Romantic Poets.

The unexpected! The more I thought about it the cleverer it became. Which should have been a Sprite warning. Each student would reveal themselves. What a finale for Creative Writing 210! I am blushing just thinking about it. I found this obscure short story. In an edition of 'Prairie Fire'. I told my secretary to cut the story in half and photocopy twenty copies. I was rushed. I didn't proofread. I was to give a presentation to the annual meeting of the Imperial Order of the Daughters of the Revolution. I am not joking, and neither are they. I had my Teaching Assistant invigilate. He still hasn't forgiven me.

The instructions were simple: Complete the short story as you perceive it.

Now the *Sprites* interfere…

My secretary cut the story in half vertically, not horizontally. My Teaching Assistant hasn't forgiven me because he still suffers from the injuries. He was never the same, psychologically. He became a stunt car driver.

It's called hysterical crying, if you must know. I am invigilating my very first final exam. And I am being very pompous and quite authoritarian about the whole ordeal. Having taken endless number of exams, it was strange and exciting to be on the enemy's side. My Sprite of course knows this. The tension in the classroom is electric. Lightning could strike at any time. In those early days, the final exam was worth 75% of the course mark. Ridiculous. I soon changed it to 20%. Course work during the term was more important.

I never felt so German. I was marching up and down the aisle, getting a closer look at human suffering. I stopped at Mark's desk. The few words scribbled on the exam booklet were wet and soggy as they smeared the page. "Mark, is there anything wrong?" He lifted his head and

WAILED.

WAILED as I supported him down the aisle of frightened students.

WAILED as I told him to meet me in the faculty lounge at three.

WAILED all the way down the corridor

Wailed across the parking lot and up the hill to the dorms.

You are so wired with fears and nerve wracked spasms that, even though you want to stop crying, you can't stop crying. Thanks to a friend's weed, Mark slowly relaxed still sniffling and snorting like an old steam engine chugging into the station. Needs fresh air. In the parking lot to amuse himself, Mark tosses a stone in the air with one hand and catches it with the other. This last stone flew high but wide. Smashed his windshield. Mark had to postpone delivering his trunk to the Bus Depot because he had accidentally packed his wallet and keys.

It was shortly after three o'clock. Knock at the faculty lounge door. A banging really with a loud rattling. Mark enters and walks to my table. When he opens his right hand, he is holding the doorknob. And some blood in a deep cut across his palm. "Mark, Go! GO to the infirmary. And then GO home. Just go! You are a danger to humanity. I will mail you the exam."

As he left, I felt sorrow for the doors between here and the infirmary. I said, "though Mark couldn't hear me, May The Sprites kindly watch over you! (but not too close) (protect yourself)."

I only did this once, but I was very proud of my Sprite. It was a most unusual class, but then so many of my classes could fall into the category of unusual. My youngest daughter was a member, and a number of the students I knew when they were being breast fed. Eighteen years later, I was in awe at the dexterity of mama nature.

I decided to check their veracity. They were constantly entering and exiting my office. So… I left a fake mid-term exam on my desk. You know absent-minded professors. I soon suspected this espionage had the questions all across the campus – even as far as The Kremlin. One question asked, "What is on page 93 of each novel?" (At least they read that much of the novels.) One question asked, "What is the middle name of each author?" One question asked, "Write a short paragraph that compares Mother Theresa and Moby Dick."

I had just explained the ruse, and was ready to hand out the real exam, when a student arrived late. I handed him the fake exam. Everyone pretended to be busy answering the questions. We watched him set his books on the floor. He grabbed the exam. Obviously, he hadn't heard. As he read each question, it was as if he kept having whip lash.

My Sprite whispered in my ear, "They thought it was real!"

Fifteen

Little did I know, but soon I would learn more than a little about the Townsend Mansion. It was haunted. Is haunted. Will always be haunted. A place where dreams were ruined, and Eden was touched by the sins of man.

It doesn't look haunted. What's left of it anyway. Ashes, some timbers, and a stone chimney standing like a tombstone. Yet standing on what once was the veranda of the mansion, you can feel a chill snake through your spine, hear the dead quiet after a scream. Demons do not haunt this place. The brutal violence of men did not cause the haunting.

The haunting is caused by a spectacular vista, a panoramic symmetry of snow-capped mountains, dark green forests, and the quiet blue crystal waters of Kootenay Lake. It is not the house that is haunted, but the land. Maybe it's the long meandering lakes. Maybe it's the mystical blue haze that dusts the mountains. Maybe it's the vagabond sun that scorches the snow caps with gold, then pink, then night. Maybe it's a million trillion stars reflected in the snow and frozen in the winter moonlight.

Maybe, simply, it's The Kootenays. A very magical place. Where the odd and occasional rainbow, tucked between the mountains and their grey blankets of clouds, has inside its pot of gold a malevolent darkness. Some ventured from the safety of their homes captured by the dream of gold and silver riches hidden in these majestic mountains. Lost. Usually lost to the mad avarice of other hunters and of course to fools gold (Pyrite). Like coal tar Johnny whose stake became a cave with a trickle of gold he chopped at his whole life. His lantern light was near the eye of elephant mountain that gazes compassionately on the rugged quests of faulty men. Then one night it wasn't lit… and never was again. Some innocent adventurers were fooled by the pictures shysters took. They hung potatoes from trees and spoke enthusiastically of the lush apple growing valleys and sold shacks as homes to the gullible and the desperate who sometimes starved during those long winters. Lost. The people of the South Wind travelled grave distances to bury the bones of their dead, here, in this sacred land where their ancestors' spirits could roam in tranquility. These First People are but ghosts to us now, as time will make ghosts of us all. If you listen, you can hear their sighs as the wind rustles through the forests of infinite trees. Lost.

You can't buy it even if you wanted too. The property. It is in arrears. No one seems interested. Not surprising as you shall see. Besides the stark ruins of the Townsend Mansion, the property is filled with weeds, mostly ugly tansies, small bushes, watch out for burs and needle thorns. Some spindly birch trees still remain. In the moonlight, the white birches seem like ghosts guarding a sacred passage. Of course, there is the blackened remains of the old mansion. Some say it was struck by lightning. Some say Halloween pranksters torched it. Some say it was the mad Baines's daughter, Isabella, out of spite. Some say demons – nobody says that any longer.

Interested in at least seeing the real estate? Once is more than enough for me. The magnet of other passions now rules my life. But if you are interested, it is the property at the bottom of the dirt road that takes you up to the abandoned Minto Mine. You can park your car there. No rentals. Four-wheel drive really is a necessity. From the parking lot you can hike to Kokanee Glacier. Wildflowers are best in early August.

By the time I ventured out along the winding North Shore road, the Townsend Mansion had already burnt to the ground many months before. The ashes were cold so to speak. The lightning rock stolen, if it was ever really there, although Trevor mentions it twice in his diary. Curiously, no photographs of the Mansion have been found as if some mystery shrouds it. But plenty pictures of the incredible vista exist. These one-dimensional pictures, usually grainy black and white and slightly blurred, cannot capture the vista's magnificent allure. I know I tried. I have seen this magnificent vista only once. No need to see it again. Probably with what I know I am afraid. Probably. Whatever was there, then, is still there – waiting. Like finding a lost civilization or being in a generation that time has passed leaving behind the rubble of crazy fashions and inexplicable notions. But I fully understand why this magnificent vista had captivated some men, so much so that they wanted to possess it. And were willing, and ignorant, in sacrificing for it so many beautiful beings.

The story of the haunting of the Townsend Mansion begins with Trevor Townsend. He discovered the stunning vista and built the stone Mansion. Master Townsend was a mechanical engineer who kept the stern wheelers running.

When not tinkering with their finicky engines, Trevor surveyed for the Canadian Pacific the vast lake system of the Kootenays. The CP railway tracks from the East ended at Portia and the Kettle Valley Railroad tracks began west to the coast at Desdemona.

Many an early English explorer loved their Shakespeare and named places along the rail line for their favourite Shakespeare characters. Of course, no Iago. Yes, a place was called Lear's Fool, but it didn't last very long. Names can kill. Only a rusted water tank remains today.

To travel from Portia to Desdemona, no roads, my friends, you could trek the hazardous mule routes or float in an elegant stern wheeler. With their splashing paddle wheels, two tall belching smoke stacks, yew panelled cabins, and a dining hall with white lace table cloths, fine Dolton China, and silversmith cutlery, the stern wheelers were a mirage rather than a reality as they plied the waters of Kootenay Lake. (Three entrees were offered even during the war. CP's Maître-dis would apologise if not feasible.)

When a stern wheeler arrived, it, merely a speck in the distance, blasted a whistle that echoed down the lake. Among the excited crowds that gathered at the docks was a skinny little man no one bothered to notice. Trevor Townsend.

It was a festival! A giant party! The arrival of a stern wheeler was rare. Crowds of citizens rushed to the docks. The two competing hotels, The Greyson and The Johnsonian, each with their own bands and banners marched to dock side to entice travelers who were waiting for the train west. $3.98 a night (does not include a hot bath). Folks from across the lake on the North Shore would row across in their canoes and dinghies. Some rowed by the family's Indian servants. Concessionaires immediately set up shop. It was a god damn holiday!

The gang planks slammed down. People and goods spilled out. Still nobody bothered to notice the shy quiet fellow in overalls and a wool cap pulled way down which didn't hide a face full of acne that had not diminished since puberty. As he picks up a heavy leather valise full of tools, he squints as he adjusts his glasses with those thick lenses. One of these days come spring, Katherine, his English war bride, would be arriving on one of these behemoths.

Work to do. Master Townsend had to recondition the marine motors. Then back to his job of surveying by horseback the North Shore. First, he crossed Kootenay Lake on the ferry from Desdemona to the North Shore. Then the road which was a narrow dirt path used by the Indians. The Quasonee (accent on Qua).

The Quasonee were rarely seen. Ghost figures, silent traders, who appeared and fled in the sudden twist of a feather in a breeze.

They had travelled most of that autumn day. His ass ached. Suddenly… Trevor's horse stopped. No, No bear. Nor a coyote. Then Trevor noticed the knoll and the clearing all the way to the beach. Either some interlopers had harvested the stand of birches or a devil wind had torn through snapping them. They lay rotting everywhere.

That's when Trevor noticed the vista.

He gasped.

Got slowly off his horse and just stood there mesmerised. So, his diary writes. It was a sunny late autumn afternoon. And the trees wore colourful costumes as if they were celebrating the arrival of a stern wheeler.

Trevor Townsend staked his claim and bought title to the land from the government agent in Desdemona. Prowling around the knoll that afternoon searching for a water source, Trevor stumbled over a pile of rocks. More than a pile of rocks. It was a wall of rocks that formed a gigantic circle of stones. Trevor could barely discern the design of the stones for the thickness of the brush. He knew, though.

The Quasonee had been here. Translated from the Quasonee, Trevor was standing in the center of their 'eternal circle of lost souls'. Thousands of rocks were used to build this large circle. A Quasonee would lay a single rock as a sign that he had been present at the silent ritual. From sometimes vast distances, the Quasonee would carry the bones of their dead and bury them here in one of the many sacred circles in this peaceful land. War was forbidden here among the many peoples of the south wind.

The lost souls could find their spirit here in this enclosure. It had to be here. Somewhere in the center of the enclosure. A lightning rock. Very, very rare. And there it was – a lightning rock. So dark blue that it appeared black. And cutting through it, streaks of white rock. It has been said that in the moon light the lightning rock glows and in the sun light it dims. Finding a lightning rock was as rare as finding a seam of gold. He would build his house, here, with these stones. And in the very center of his house, hidden, would be this lightning rock. The Gods of the Quasonee would be pleased, and benefits would descend upon Trevor's house.

Katherine had arrived that spring and three long years later Trevor Townsend had completed his stone mansion. The stone mansion watched from its perch on the knoll the ever-changing hues of the vista. And the vista watched the lives of the people who chose to live beyond its radiance.

But it was a house of the dead. Death lived here. All three babies, boys, were still born. His wife, Katherine, died of consumption during one long brutal winter. Curiously, no one knew where he buried the ashes of his loved ones. No one.

Master Trevor Townsend lived alone even when there were people around him. Occasionally, his older brother Terence would come to visit. Trevor lived out his days in the ticks and chimes of his loneliness. He continually checked the great grandfather clock in the hallway that Katherine had shipped all the way from England. Trevor was afraid when the pendulum stopped swinging so would he stop living.

But he wasn't alone. He had his vista.

Trevor Townsend aged quickly in that cold stone house. He would never leave. Never! He preferred the ghosts of his family to the Jell-O of an old folk's home.

He grew quite senile babbling about some dark rock inside him. His diary entries had lapsed long ago. Some towns folk felt empathy for this pioneer, others, jealous of him, sneered with the irony of a man whose vision was so hazy that he couldn't really see his vista.

A lawyer, Zackery Innes, now enters our story. And evil has entered this beautiful house with its innocent vista. But maybe not so innocent. True beauty holds a treacherous power to possess and be possessed. Beauty and its brilliance are often a curse. Vilified. Hated.

Zackery Innes didn't get dressed in the morning. He adorns himself. Cuff links – check. Tie clasp – check. Pocket watch chain – check. Three peaked silk handkerchief – check. Silver belt buckle – check. Wedding ring (loose) – check. Law school graduation ring (tight) – check. But the piece-de-resistance is the flowing mound of silky black hair combed (after a gel) straight back. You hardly notice his birth defect. His right leg is shorter than his left. So, his preening strut is quite funny. With a hat and a cane, Zackery Innes could be a version of Charlie Chaplin's the little tramp.

All of this is just snide gibberish, because of his most prominent attribute – a booming voice. Symphonic. Judges love him. Juries love him. Clients love him. Everyone else hates him, voice and all. He's a circus barker. A snake oil hawker. He sells all the law he has bent or at least dented. His booming voice shuddered the rafters of the Anglican Church where he was from time to time asked to provide the Sunday homily. I am sure to the Lord's chagrin. But the congregation loved the theatrical shenanigans of Zachery Innes rather than Dean Baines's tedious monotony. I am surprised that he didn't shatter the embarrassed figures in the stain glass windows.

Zackery Innes was Trevor Townsend's lawyer. You can fill in the blanks. Zackery had become utterly infatuated with the vista. Zackery found any excuse to visit Trevor whose reality shrank as his dementia expanded. Zackery must possess this land. Own it. One night, Zackery had Trevor sign some normal court papers. Quite procedural, really. So, when Trevor died of consumption, like his Katherine, the will read that for one dollar Zackery Innes was awarded possession of Trevor Townsend's designated land and mansion. Trevor died as he lived, quietly, absorbed in his vista, the painful beauty of being alive.

Affronted! Disgusted! Appalled! was the town, but also Zackery Innes' own family who felt the needles and stings of the town's resentment. Rumours like weeds sprouted in many neighbours' minds that Zackery had smothered Trevor with Katherine's needle point pillow. Terence Townsend appealed, but the legal wrangling muted all protestations. Shunned. The Zackery victory parade consisted of no marching bands and no floats. Just Zackery waving to nobody looking. No more invitations to preach in the Anglican Church. Even the stain glass figures turned their heads away. His wife divorced him. His children despised him. None, not one, of the family would ever set foot in that damned house of ill-gotten gains.

It didn't help Zackery Innes's social redemption when he was over heard saying: "It is all legal. Anyway, Trevor was so demented he couldn't appreciate the vista. With his dementia, Trevor needed a good lawyer."

Zackery Innes never became accustomed to being shunned but being ignored riled him. Constantly, Zackery reminded himself that he got what he wanted and no one else could possess it. Sir Zackery Innes died – I guess – of a heart attack sitting in his rocking chair while watching the sun set on his vista. A court reporter found him months later. In the eyes of the town, Zackery Innes had died long ago. Zackery was not invited to his youngest daughter's wedding. She held the festivities on the adjacent property, so her father could see and hear but not touch.

When Zackery Innes's last will and testament was read out loud in the magistrate's court, the packed court room erupted in laughter. The land and mansion were donated to the Anglican Church as residence for the Dean and his family. Everyone wondered if Saint Peter and even God himself could be bribed by a petty small-town lawyer. Might want to check the Book of Job.

Would the evil forces be placated? We will see as our story enters its climax and as I enter the story with the Baines family, since I often talked to the youth group. Reverend Baines loved English literature, especially the Holmes sagas. Besides Charles Baines, father, there was his wife, Marcia, his eldest daughter, Isabella, eighteen, his youngest, Emily, thirteen, and his son, Daemon, eleven. A student of mine has yet to appear. But he soon will. I so wanted a happy ending.

Sooner than I thought.

Tim Livingston at eighteen graduated from high school but didn't know what to do next. So, he joined the Canadian Army. Hoping to shoot somebody like a Frog or some Ottawa brass. Timothy's life were guns, girls, guys, guzzling beer, gambling, gut hits and grappling. Four years later, appalled at the waste he had created, Tim left Cold Lake army base. He enrolled as a liberal arts major. Timothy Livingston was adopted by the Baines family. Tim even joined the Anglican Church youth group. Isabella had nothing to do with it. He never missed a meeting and some he even planned.

The Sunday of the tragedy happened to be Easter Sunday. The youth group was having a picnic on the Baines beach. Isabella and Timothy were becoming concerned. Marcia and Charles Baines were late returning from a satellite church service. Reverend Baines and his wife would not be returning. A chain snapped. That chain was the major latch holding a Caterpillar Backhoe Loader to a trailer. The Backhoe Loader smashed into the Baines car crushing it and its occupants. Isabella, eighteen, was now responsible for her sister, Emily, thirteen, and her brother, Daemon, eleven. Timothy Livingston, twenty-two, helped whenever he could, which was often.

Timothy Livingston blasted into my office, slamming the door behind him. "I will call you back," I said, as I replaced the phone. Timothy was pale and frantic, shaking. "I'm going crazy, CRAZY!" "I'm glad you have decided to join the rest of us." I got Tim to sit down but not to calm down. When I heard what had happened to him and Isabella, I was pale and frantic, shaking. I was already sitting down.

"Late last night, Isabella and I were laying together by the fire place. We were naked cuddling each other. We had sex. Then we heard someone on top of us, breathing. We sat up, screaming. No one was there, but. But the rocking chair was swaying back and forth, back and forth. Which could be anything causing it. The seat of the rocking chair was depressed as if someone was sitting in it watching us. Isabella was chocked trembling with fear. I got up and kicked the rocking chair across the room. It still swayed. I picked it up and pitched it outdoors. I had planned to spend the weekend with Isabella, and even though I wanted to get the hell out of there, I stayed. The next morning I was in the upstairs bathroom, shaving, when the bathroom was filled with hideous laughter. I have never heard anything like it. I looked out the window and there was Emily sitting on the swing, just staring up at me. I didn't finish shaving. I headed for the kitchen where I had left my coat, keys, and wallet. Before I could get the hell out of there, a cup and saucer flew across the kitchen crashing into the refrigerator."

I told Tim not to worry. He had experienced Poltergeist. The teenage daughter, Emily, into puberty is only protecting what is left of the family. Isabella. "You are seen as an interloper stealing Isabella away. What would she and Daemon do? They would be abandoned. I know someone who can help you and the Baines family. But you must never enter that house again. You are safe if you are willing to do that. Tell no one. Never speak of this again. To no one," I said.

I introduced Tim to Father Hansen. Father Hansen had studied exorcism with a Hungarian Jesuit, Father Milos Jasinski. The three Baines children left Desdemona for Vancouver. A small delegation from the Vatican and a smaller delegation from Canterbury arrived in Desdemona to purify the premises with a book of ancient prayers. Very secretive. Father Hansen never spoke of it again.

The Townsend mansion and its lands were abandoned. The Anglican Church Hierarchy and the local board of governors tried unsuccessfully to sell the property. No one was interested.

Some months later, the mansion burnt to the ground. And the lightning rock – if it ever was there – disappeared.

Thanks to the Quasonnee Council of Elders; The University Archivist, Ted Nugget; The Budapest Public Library; The Vatican Library's Father Hansen's papers; Ronald Ballwell's "A Brief History of the Stern Wheeler in the Kootenays."

I wouldn't plan on driving out to see the vista. It doesn't exist any longer and you will be disappointed. Across the breast of the far mountains BC Hydro has planted steel towers to carry high tension electrical power to the coast. Forestry has cut roads back and forth through the woods that still exist after the forest fire during the summer of 2011. A two-lane highway cuts through the land. The Government has built a boat ramp and parking lot. At the bottom of the incline, A Stop N Shop convenience store is open 24/7. Next to the Stop N Shop is a rural fire and rescue station. Trevor Townsend Fire Brigade Number Three.

Sixteen

I worked six summers as a desk clerk at the English Village Motor Lodge. In those six summers, I saw every type of human being God has permitted a few seconds of existence. Worked for a manager whose six billion neuron cells burned cynical. He could have been raised in a rat family. Scurrying here, scurrying there, nibble, nibble, everywhere.

He was also a flippin' hypocrite. "Don't trust anyone driving a Cadillac." "That's ridiculous! You can't make a general statement like that!"

The very next day. The Very! I was on the morning shift when I saw this Cadillac drive out of the motor inn. I stood there – stunned. The double bed was tied to the roof, the chester drawers and leisure chair were sticking out of the trunk, the television set, paintings, drapes, bed tables, luggage rack, pillows, sheets, blankets, shower curtain were all jammed in the back seat. They left the souvenir ash tray on the floor where they tried to rip up the carpet that was glued to the floor. They told the RCMP that they thought the furnishing were included in the price of the room. The Cadillac had Texas license plates.

I have a nugget of idealism still left, but the rest of me is pure rancid cynicism. Thanks to the English Village Motor Lodge and Texans in general. And it doesn't help that my father's family are Texans.

Or for that matter, how about the drunken guest who was climbing and clinging to the outside glass and frames of the glassed-in stairwell to the second floor. Cursing. His luggage strewn across the pavement that he had previously dropped. "God damn fuckin' stairs!" I am sure the desperate fly banging himself senseless against the window pain is yelling the same curses.

My wife has never liked anything I have ever written, creatively, except my speech when I retired. It ends this book. So, you have the chance to skip right to the end. She did. Whereas I was a wiz-bang teacher, my creative words always died upon the page. Literary anaesthesia. I guess I am just one of those quirky weird persons too unusual to be believed. Even I shake my head in disbelief 'did that actually happen'. Maybe I have lived in the Kootenays much too long where 'normal' has never been convincingly defined.

I have all the pieces, but not the puzzle.

Seventeen

We ventured west to teach at a small catholic university when we had never taught a single class. Venturing not by covered wagon. Nor stagecoach. Neither of us could ride a horse. Nix, the Canadian Pacific sleeper from Toronto. Too expensive. We were wallet poor (small, catholic, and a university). We rode west on a Ford Galaxy 500 – my first car and second love. The trunk was full of our stuff – mostly books (small, catholic, university). We were newlyweds. Obviously – in case she reads this – my first love. We left behind many of the things we love in the hopes of finding between us a new love.

We road into a small town of heritage buildings, vintage homes, and antique ways. At first introductions, the people seemed aloof and docile to the weary ways of the world. They cleverly hid their craziness. Soon, like them, you are on Kootenay time. You have forgotten you have a watch and just guess at the time. Especially during the long days of summer that melts calendars. An eight o'clock appointment would occur somewhere between 7:40 and 8:20.

Doctor Trent Middleditch – the only optometrist in town. Man, could that man talk. Mostly about the National Geographic. He loved the Geographic. Soon, somehow through the maze of chatter you were actually talking about yourself instead of turtles in the Galapagos. Unfortunately, he hated optometry. Wouldn't you? All day long all you read was **E P Z O M T**. He often threatened to project **F U C K Y U**. Never did though. Appointment times were either morning or afternoon, so you did quite a bit of waiting and flipping through National Geographic. Cleverly, T. Middleditch screwed only 25-watt bulbs in all the lamps, so, by the time you actually got to see the doctor you could barely see.

After three years (at the most), we promised, we would pack up our stuff, more boxes of books, and race back to our families in the East. Hoping that the lazy mumble of our soft west coast accent would be understood. And a loving return to loud nasal shouting, possible. But it was not to be.

I became enchanted with the Kootenays (my fourth love). There is no other place like it in the whole world. Some places in this world are real with bits of fantasy, whereas the Kootenays are fantasy with pieces of reality. But you must see it, feel it, need it, wish it, then it is yours forever. And you will take it with you into the next realm. Living just down the block is the Wizard of Oz who has in his parlour a pair of ruby slippers forgotten by a young girl who was not ready yet.

No, I have not been forgotten by number three love. I am a bit of a rascal and the West loves rascals. Universities don't. It was a miracle that I survived. I was saved from the academic wrangling by grandma Wilson's old fashion fudge recipe and the incandescent power of my third love: teaching.

It took my wife a long, long, long, Kootenay time, and two daughters, to feel at home in these quiet valleys. I don't want to ask her if she finally has a home here. I assume she has. But don't ask her about tacks. She remembers driving herself to town to purchase tacks. NO tacks. Tacks are on order. Tacks in two weeks when the train arrives. No one offered to loan her a couple of tacks. In Chicagoland, there were thousands and thousands of tacks in huge bins. Whenever she became frustrated, she would once again attack tacks.

The first day blues. The narrow twisting road into town swerved up then down then back and after another swerve more forth. Even before we arrived, we needed a drink, now it was imperative. The Broad board Beach Inn was open. Why or how, I don't know. I ordered a martini; my wife ordered a Manhattan. We both got gin and tonics. My drink had an olive in it; my wife's drink a cherry. We didn't inquire. Afraid it was some tribal rite.

We found out that the men smoking in a group by the Post Office were Remittance men paid monthly by their bourgeois or aristocratic families to stay out of England because they were an embarrassment to a name or a title. Like a pregnant whore or conversion to Catholicism! Rich California families continued this tradition in the 1960s when hippy bodies filled the valleys around the town. There was weed in them their hills. Nobody prospected for gold or silver any longer.

There were three naked grannies on the lawn in front of the court house. Well, not totally naked. They were wearing big black gum boots. Police officers were hosing them down. They were Russian, Doukhobors, Sons of Freedom cult members protesting their right to live free of government edicts. They have fought for their rights across the globe ever since the time of the Tzars.

We were told not to worry, because they don't bomb any longer. And since we are not Russian, they won't burn our house down. Their world is fading into the world of 1965, but they will never forget that night. That night is every night. That day is every day. The night the Government sent the RCMP into their community and snatched their children from their beds. The children were imprisoned behind a steel fence enclosure in New Denver for years. The parents could touch their children's hands through the metal fence on some Sunday afternoons if the children behaved themselves.

Why? Because the Doukhobors refused to send their children to public school. They demanded the right to educate their own children. They also refused to pay taxes. Their anger is still there beneath the lush fruits, fresh vegetables, warm breads, and colourful jams at their Saturday morning market. In 1965, yes, but not any longer. Not only do runners become exhausted, but so too causes.

One old black and white photograph captures the Doukhobor way. Two hefty women pulling a plow.

I once asked a Doukhobor grand mother why she had come back to school. "So you can teach me the words to tell them of my anger." She went on to sue the government.

What had our fates driven us into? When you are young, you don't think of tomorrow; come to think of it, you don't think of tomorrow, especially when you are old.

We rented a house on the lake. 60 bucks a month. We were paying 240 in Washington (and no view). A summer house. No insulation. There were woodpecker holes and cheap pine cracks, so, when the wind blew off the lake, the house sounded like an accordion played by a crazy creole from the bayou.

The house was jerry-built by putting room after room like blocks on a string, so, the only bedroom was at one end of the house and the only bathroom was at the opposite end – about a kilometre and a half hike. You had to run fast for fear of freezing to death. I was always afraid my pee would pump out in chunks. Only the kitchen was an ice-skating rink. Everywhere else was covered with ornate Persian rugs. Only one baby grand piano, although there was a foot pumped organ. Cupboards full of fine bone china. Antiques everywhere. You were afraid to sit down without making a bid.

The two sisters who owned this windy accordion were quite wealthy. They were in England settling an estate. One sister was oblivious to money, so when she died, she saw clouds; the other sister was obsessed with money, so when she died, she saw giant ants eating her dollars. A very merry English relationship.

No matter how hard you tried, you would scream when you hit the kitchen floor.

Come to think of it, there was new construction. A tool shed. It sat between the bedroom and a very sharp curve in the North Shore road. It was constantly being wrecked as drivers lost control of their vehicles. Colonel Karnal, our neighbour, told me each time the insurance company rebuilt the shed, it got stronger and stronger. Just a better target. Each night we went to bed in terror we would wake up with a Volkswagen in the middle of our bed with an uptight German Lutheran couple who were adverse to a foursome.

It was our very first Christmas in our new town. I asked Colonel Karnal where you would buy a Christmas tree. He looked at me then looked up the mountain side. I cut my very first Christmas tree stumbling up the mountain and sliding with the tree bumping me all the way down. Snow filled my boots; my toque was lost somewhere. I set the tree by the grand piano. We had no cash (small, catholic, university). So, we had no lights, no ornaments. What we had were stacks and stacks of grammar exercises. Some antiquated teaching technique from the nineteenth century. Everyone hated them. They would cease in the new year. In fact, there were to be many changes. And many uproars. I couldn't believe the uproar I caused when I decided to teach the Beatles 'Eleanor Rigby'. So, we decorated the tree with grammar exercises. It looked beautiful. No, it didn't. But we were in love.

The next morning when we got up, the little tree had died sometime during the night. It shed all its needles and one dead pinecone. I still believe the grammar exercises killed it. Up the mountain I went, in fact two more times. Colonel Karnal thought I was clear cutting.

We were invited to the annual New Year's Eve party traditionally held at Myrtle MacIntosh's digs. I guess we were officially accepted after our initiation passage through high tea. I thought it would be Earl Grey and scones. High tea is cucumber sandwiches (no crusts) and sherry. Lots and lots of sherry. The English know how to spend an afternoon. Lenard MacIntosh was a hen-pecked pip-squeak married to none other than that kettle drum Myrtle MacIntosh. Bang! Bang! Bang! What a gossip – complete with loudmouth and wild gestures. She spied on everybody. Bang! Bang! She lived next door to us and we all lived in the middle of the town's English community which, in 1965, when we arrived, was dying out. It was becoming their last HURRAH!

I was in Overweatea fingering seductively the zucchinis when I suddenly sneezed. When I got home, it had already been reported that I was coming down with a cold. But hated? Myrtle? No! No! No! Myrtle concocted the most luscious desserts you have ever salivated over. I would sell my soul – if I had one – for just one slice of her chocolate flan.

Lenard MacIntosh was already in the closet when we arrived at the New Year's Eve gala. Myrtle allowed him one bender a year. New Year's Eve.

Colonel Karnal was our guide through the characters living their last days in the English community that, like the native culture, would be gone in a decade, even less. Colonel Karnal wore all his military medals. He clanked when he walked. A stiff walk with arthritis in his joints. He needed a cane to hobble around.

War was the best time in his life. After the war, everything else was quite dull. He was a bachelor who wooed the ladies but didn't win them over. He loved the war too much. His dwellings were full of world war memorabilia. The latest purchase was from Scotland: an eighteenth-century canon with three canon balls. It was to be shot off after midnight.

You never really saw Colonel Karnal's face because he owns a huge moustache and heavy bushy eyebrows. No beard, but giant side burn whiskers. None ever mowed. He has an impressive carriage and a durable winter sleigh pulled by his two geldings: Gypsy and Rabbi. He owned two German Shepherd dogs, Hitler and Stalin. Along with the Colonel, they looked quite mean, but were really rather mellow. The three of them always crashed our high Tea get-togethers.

Colonel Karnal never shot anybody, at least intentionally. Gun battles were for bravado at the Legion Hall. Colonel Karnal drove the brass around battlefields not into them. He was their pimp. A very successful pimp, rising in the ranks. He could always find food and ladies to fill the needs of the upper crust militarists. Only twice did Colonel Karnal have to dive into a ditch to save himself and his cargo from Gerry strafing in their Ardo Ar Two Forties. Blew one jeep to hell, ruining a wham bang picnic. One memorable picnic for a three-star general and two lovely mamma mia and a full basket of wine and eats happened on a secluded beach, while they watched as if the battle was a movie:

The Allied Bombardment of a Sicilian town. Usually the brass died of cirrhosis of the liver, not battle fatigue. They killed with paper and pen. Maybe they have their own trenches in the chilly statistics of the battlefield. So said Colonel Karnal before he told us about the…

…Casualty of a much-decorated pimp. Colonel Karnal's heart was broken, and when a heart is broken, it seldom is repaired. Because of his rank (and owed debts), his war bride was given preference. She was on the first ship of war brides to cross the Atlantic from South Hampton. When the ship docked in New York, she vanished. She had used him as he had used so many others. After that, all women, all, were Eves.

Colonel Karnal provided us with high tea biographies of the guests we would meet at Myrtle's New Year's Eve bash. He discussed their facades as well as their human predicaments. He meant stories. 'Human Stories'. Actually, standing there amongst all these English souls, I suddenly realized they could all be characters in the universe of a Dickens novel. Each guest could be squeezed inside one long involved Dicksonian sentence that reveals they are neither guilty nor innocent of the deeds they have perpetrated. And why is that? Because of the grace fiction allows. Unlike judges and priests, authors can excuse any act a character can commit with just a flick of a pen. Unlike characters, people should be so lucky!

There, of course, was Lenard MacIntosh. Inebriated in the front closet. I opened the closet door, handed him a bottle of whiskey, wished him a happy 1966 (YEAH! YEAH!) and quietly shut the closet door. Never saw Lenard the whole year until I once again opened on New Year's Eve that closet door. Sober, I wondered if he ever took to the closet on an ordinary day when the world got too crusty for his constitution. Now and then I could use such a closet.

There of course was Abigail Bingington. Of the North Shore Bingingtons. One hardware store. One sawmill. One honeycomb burner. And by default, bourgeois status. She, the Dowager, wanted desperately to be royalty. Impossible. Sir Bingington was a gangly man with excessively long arms and legs and a nose to match. He was also at one time a Remittance man. Impossible. Lady Bingington walked and talked like a Patton tank.

Lady Bingington loved her jewels. She never could decide which ones to wear, so, she wore them all. No bear could hug with the intensity of Lady Bingington. Because of all those jewels' sharp edges, I was wearing a thick woollen vest, so I didn't bleed to death. And because of the light hitting that blaze of jewels, wherever Lady Bingington harrumphed, she flashed.

Dickens would have loved how Lady Abigail Bingington of the North Shore Bingington's story ended. She wheedled and wheedled her wheedling way onto the guest list of the last stern wheeler trip – the farewell voyage of the S.S. Nasookin. A fierce august storm suddenly leaped across the head of Elephant Mountain and dashed viciously across Kootenay Lake. Taken by surprise, the S.S. Nasookin sank, just a kilometre or so from completing its final journey at the docks in Desdemona. Her maid yelled at Lady Bingington to leave her jewels behind and climb the stairs still upright but slanting. But Lady Bingington could not leave without her jewels. The maid survived; Lady Bingington didn't. She couldn't have lived without her jewels – anyway.

At her funeral, not one of the ladies, out of respect, wore any ornamentation. Lady Bingington died the Bingington way: drown grasping two or three of her more expensive necklaces in her tight little fist. Divers found the rest of her jewels in the stateroom dresser. Mr. Bingington donated the entire collection to the town museum. The collection is stored in a cardboard box stashed in the museum storage room marked 'Lady Abigail Bingington Effects'. I haven't seen the spectre myself, but I've been told that if you row out to the spot where the Nasookin sank, and if the water is placid, and if it is dusk, you can see her face deep in the water. One hand with a clutch of necklaces is raised toward the surface.

We were introduced to Lord and Lady Dexter with pomp and flare. A little more flare than pomp. Circumstance had not been quite so suave to the Lord and Lady. Poor investments, actually disasters, in Lloyds of London, lost them their fortunes. Their ships kept sinking along with their prestige. Lady Dexter was seen wearing the same formal attire as last year's queen's knighthood investiture. They had only their title left which to the English still possessed a highly prized significance. So, especially, here in the Kootenays they were treated as the local royalty with obligatory pretence and a whimsy of pity. Such fanfare, except for Abigail who was exceedingly jealous! It was like a wonderful game of clue – Lord Dexter in the library with a kitchen knife. I kissed Lady Dexter's hand – surprisingly coarse and quite greasy from the breaded turnips. who, before I could remove my lips from her wrist, immediately informed me that she and her consort were the very next day travelling south for the winter. Bon Voyage! No, not really. Colonel Karnal had told us 'traveling south for the winter' actually meant staying in his brother's apartment above a garage in Yakamaw Washington.

In the hallway next to the stairs, Ted Stallworth and Ed Talbert were arguing about arguing. They were always arguing. They loved to argue. They had been arguing for over fifty years. They were born on the same day, and if they could have spoken, would have argued from their adjoining bassinets. They just cried at each other.

And lamented their fate (blaming each other). They were both prospectors who never found an ounce of gold or silver or for that matter any seam of fool's gold. So, they took their expertise in not finding riches inside mountains and became government agents in the office of the Chamber of Mines and Land Registry.

Not to mislead you. The job sounds safe, but nothing was safe in those days. A lucky prospector was shot by his partner right in front of the Chamber of Mines. The very next day, the murderous prospector had his throat slit and his body pitched off a train as it clattered over the Kettle Valley trestles. In the prospector's luggage, the killers found only bags of gravel. The night before, some whore got the loot and found some gravel. One rich fuck. One week later, voluptuous with bullion, said maiden married a traveling preacher man. They had seven children. Go and multiply. Boy did they ever. Of course, the fat stash help build quite a church. I heard the preacher man shot two or three intruders to keep his loot safe. So, what I am saying here, is…Ted and Ed were…

…Losers, no, not really. They married two very agreeable sisters. The gals were tough in a smart sort of way. They encouraged Ted and Ed's every argument. It kept the boys out of trouble. The boys were prone to drink. If prone means to fall over backwards dead drunk. As luck would have it or not have it, the gals bought themselves a pub – The Ballyhoo.

Ted and Ed built their cottages beside one another on a North Shore embankment. The gals insisted that if so, they were to plant a hedge between the properties. They could still argue but not kill each other. Over the years, the hedge grew thick and high and tangled unbelievably. It was unprovable. No blossoms, no thorns, no seeds. Insects hated it. Besides it was ugly. Even with all the verbal rancour, the hedge kept the peace.

Exceptional. Hot August afternoon. As if God had left the oven door open. Ed set up his lawn chair, and beside his lawn chair, Ed carefully placed his cooler full of ice-cold beer. With a bevy of beer already sloshing around in his gut, a large straw hat carefully adjusted, Ed drifted into a boozy reverie. Luckily, Ed didn't know what was happening on the other side of the hedge.

Furious! Be sot with acrimony! Ted did everything, said everything, thought everything in terms of conspiracies to ruin him. Like that large cotton wood stump, sorry, that fuckin' cotton wood stump. A year ago, Ted had 'timbered' the rotten giant, rotten to its baneful core. Since then he has warred against the stump to dislodge it. It was resilient to fire and choruses of "God! Damn! Jesus! Christs! I Want My Lawn Back!" that's what he said.

Ted stole them from the Chamber of Mines warehouse. The stump would be shattered. Ted dug a hole underneath the stump. He shoved into the hole not one but two sticks of dynamite.

The explosion was mighty!

But the stump didn't shatter. Add 'dang blasted' to the chorus of curses. Upward into the air shot the stump like a rocket. Slowly it tilted to the right. Oh, good lord! Over Ed's property. Then it suddenly, the stump, plummeted downward. Then the crash and then the scream! Ed sat up really quickly from his snooze. Why had a stump landed on top of Ed's now squashed cooler? Why was a stump sitting next to his lawn chair? Why was the stump smoking? In his drunken sleep teased stupor, he couldn't figure anything out. Maybe, the Mrs. suggested, he not drink so much in the hot sun. Ed decided he was using too much gypsum fertilizer!

I checked my watch. It was twenty minutes past midnight. Maybe they were on English time. I decided not to ask Myrtle since she probably controlled time too. Myrtle then bellowed "It is officially 1966. I guess they didn't want to rush things." So French. Everyone stopped. Everyone took a deep breath. And together said one loud "RAHHHHHH!!!!!" And from inside the closet, you heard a squeaky squeal r a h h h h h. And everyone went home.

Except the men. We headed for Colonel Karnal's back yard where he had set up his eighteenth-century canon. Ready to fire. And welcome 1966.

I noticed the canon was aimed toward an Osprey nest. It was too late to say anything. The fuse was lit. As Colonel Karnal stepped aside, his stiff foot nudged the canon platform ever so slightly.

A thunderous bang as the canon ball sailed toward the propane tank inside Colonel Karnal's chicken coop. There was an even louder thunderous bang as the canon ball exploded the propane tank.

Fried chickens filled the air. Fried chickens everywhere. At least a hundred, maybe more – I didn't have time to count with chickens falling from the sky. Men were screaming and running and running and screaming. Fried chickens plopping and whopping frenzied spectators. Colonel Karnal had fried chicken for weeks. Hitler and Stalin were ecstatic with this manna from the heavens. They once again believed in a god, if dogs don't or do deities. I was just glad to be alive as I pulled a fried chicken off my head.

I kept the fried chicken that hit me on the head to show my wife or she wouldn't believe me. Then, again, she also thought she could just drive into town and buy some tacks.

Eighteen

Memories are like the pieces of coloured glass in a kaleidoscope. Gently nudge the tube and the pieces of coloured glass form a lovely design. These designs are constantly changing. Sometimes subtly, sometimes dramatically. Suddenly, the pieces of coloured glass lose their colour. Each piece becomes a part of a picture of some moment in your memory. Only the pieces of coloured glass know why we remember; why we forget? Why when we age our memories yellow and fade like old photographs in a dusty album? Why do some memories torment forever? Why do some memories always delight? Why do they curiously appear and then just as mysteriously disappear? Hold the pieces of coloured glass in your hand and you hold yourself. I don't believe in a soul. But if you must have a soul, maybe this could be a soul. What would you want to be your very last memory before you exit into the endless night? This chosen memory you would take with you into eternity as the totality of your life.

We are our memories; our memories are us.

Tea and Sympathy and Big Boobs

It was a 'nice' day. Warm, I guess for September. The leaves hadn't bothered to change – yet. Or even for that matter select a few to start the fall. All and all a rather boring day. That's why I had decided to walk from the Dog N Suds to the university. The day was about to become not quite so boring.

I was passing Doctor Anton Sadler's rented house when suddenly the Ph.D. himself and his wife Celeste appeared on their rented front porch. Waving! Yelling! Something about having tea. What could I do? Bleed some excuse all over their rented sidewalk.

Doctor Anton Sadler, Ph.D., was a mistake. A big mistake. The university hiring committee wrote to him presently in Cairo that his resume had been accepted and requested an interview. He suddenly appeared on campus, assuming he had a position. He spoke Egyptian, French, and English with a heavy Oxford accent. Doctor Anton Sadler, Ph.D., was a one hundred percent Grade A academic. He could write a thesis in a slaughterhouse. The students thought he was so dull that he had died years ago and that his corpse was teaching the class. Never a mean word. Everyone was doing fine until…

…until the grades were posted. 'A' and 'B' were not in his alphabet. Mistake. Big Mistake. Before the Administration could fire him, Doctor Anton Sadler, Ph.D., and his bosomy wife Celeste landed their magic carpet somewhere back east – not far east enough for the hiring committee. The tea stain I left on their rented couch is still there. I think.

Sitting on their rented couch, I was enjoying a cup of Earl Grey tea and these very crispy cookies. One bite and they crumbled everywhere. They were small so I stuffed the whole cookie in my mouth. I looked like a glutton.

Staring at me and counting the cost of cleaning their rented couch… I hadn't even started destroying their rented couch… I kept thinking why hadn't the leaves started to fall? I was becoming desperate. Why not ask them about leaves in Egypt? But what if they don't have leaves in Egypt. They certainly have crispy cookies! I gobbled another cookie. Missed. The end disintegrated. I could feel Celeste looking at all the crumbs stuck to my lips. This was social torture. By the second cup of Earl Grey tea, I had used up all the superficial questions I could think of. I did learn they have leaves in Egypt. Celeste saw them but would never rake them. The afternoon was not a total loss.

Then a topic suddenly loomed in my brain. It was so obvious why had I missed it? Probably because I was lulled by their soft voices. And of course, sitting in a bed of crumbs hoping they didn't keep rented pet pigeons.

"What is your opinion of the Arab Jewish conflict?"

Doctor Sadler leaps from his chair, nearly upset a plate of those crumbly crispy cookies who didn't even have a napkin to hide under. I had used them all. Screaming, gesturing wildly, reddening in the face, Doctor Sadler, Ph.D., screeched his vehemence against the blood thirsty Jews. I sat stunned with a damned cookie half-way toward my mouth.

That's when Celeste Sadler, his Mrs., leaps from her chair. She was also screaming. She rips down her blouse. I can still vividly remember the blouse pattern of purple begonias. Mrs. Sadler had no bra on. I could tell that immediately. She trusts her large breasts toward me.

"Do you see these breasts?"

I said meekly, "Yes, I do!" Hoping this was the end of the eye exam.

"They fed three sons. I would be a proud mother if they would all die killing Jews."

That's when I spilled my tea down my crotch and onto their rented couch.

As I stumbled down their rented walk, a leaf hit me in the head. Ouch!

The vice-president of the university, who I thought was a noodle head, asked me in the hallway if I thought Dr and Mrs. Sadler would be appropriate guests for the monthly meet and greet faculty dinner. I thought they would be exceptional! But be sure and ask them about the Arab/Jewish conflict. But be sure and have plenty of napkins available. He was such a noodle head that he didn't ask why.

Two days after the faculty dinner, a memo arrived in all our mailboxes. The memo was from the vice-president announcing that the meet and greet faculty dinners would be suspended for the remainder of the term.

The Girl with the Butterfly Tattoo

The month of January is like eating a fried egg without a yoke. Is the darkest of all the months. Even the snow that falls in flakes of white becomes a shade of grey. For this winter world, the only paint can available is metallic grey. The winter sun, probably out of embarrassment, hides behind thick almost fat grey clouds. Built with beige brick and grey cement, MacGregor Hall always reflects the passing season. The third-floor corridor was a morgue of gloomy shadows.

I was sauntering down the corridor. I don't exactly know what it means to saunter. But I was sauntering. I am sure of it. I was wearing my new Christmas sweater. We were to attend an art school gallery opening that very evening. I was heading for the locked closet where the TV carts are stored. I was to cue two tapes for an early morning class.

Near the closet were two workman, dirty tee shirts and soiled jeans, standing on short metal stilts to easily repair damaged ceiling tiles. "Clever!" I duly reported. They just glared down at me as if guards to some gangster sanctum.

I am on one knee by the TV cart when flying around the corner is Sue Cleary. She flits everywhere like a hummingbird. She is always laughing, always excited at whatever commotion she is causing. Sue Cleary is effervescence, just cork popped.

I hadn't seen her since the winter term started. We new-year-wished each other. "Christmas sweater, I bet." "Yep!" "Bet you can't guess what I got… A tattoo!" "A TATTOO!" "You want to see it?" "Sure!"

Sue pulls up her sweater. Shoves down her skirt. There around her navel is a large yellow and black butterfly. "It's Beautiful!" And off Sue flies chasing that white rabbit.

I glance up at the two workmen. Two stunned faces stare down at me. "And gentlemen… They pay me extravagantly for the privilege."

Auntie Joan's Flaming Gladiolas

Emaciated. Ascetic. Immaculate. That's what a Reverend Dean of the Anglican Church of Desdemona should look like. One Charles Baines. But Charlie looked more like a used car salesman than a minister of the cloth. Though there were some interesting similarities there. Reverend Dean Baines was chubby. Always was chubby. Was chubby as a foetus. Many too many bake sales sponsored by the Saint Ruth of Sicily Ladies Society kept him chubby.

The bake sales help pay the expenses of a missionary in Zululand. Hush, now. Most of the expenses were liquor. At least huge vats and oak barrels. The good-hearted missionary built the natives a distillery. The tribe is quite wealthy now. And they eat people only on every other Tuesdays. Mrs. Mildred Middleditch, caught between menopause and total insanity, felt that Saint Ruth was calling to her to assist in the missionary's beneficial works. What misfortune! Gasp! And the very day, too, that Mildred was to leave she fell down the choir loft stairs and broke her hip. Gasp! I still believe Saint Ruth of Sicily pushed her. Hush, now.

It droned on and on and on. Reverend Charles Baines voice. When he spoke, you couldn't tell the difference between a 'P' and a 'C'. He coughs in drone (folks have heard them), and some of the more ribald laity wonder what his farts sound like. In the Anglican Liturgy, Anglican Ministers do not fart. But if by chance through – say – a bowl of Mildred's chilli, minister Baines should fart he would instantly die a hellish death or become a Lutheran.

The quality of a Dean Baines Sunday sermon was determined by the number of parishioners who fell asleep or how many hymnals fell from the pews. On the feast day of Saint Ruth of Sicily, four parishioners fell out of their pews onto the floor. Just two, God bless, had concussions. Oh, the choir mistress broke her collar bone. Dean Baines told his adoring wife that he had to tone down his sermons – too many of his flock were being flushed with frenzies.

Some (they were Pharisees) waited religiously for a Baines bomb. A weird analogy or an outlandish Biblical interpretation. On the Sunday of the Immaculate Conception, Reverend Baines told the congregation that the reason for the Immaculate Conception was the lack of condoms in Biblical times. Only the Romans could afford rubbers made of pig skin. Dean Baines kept calling the feast day 'The Immaculate Contraception'. Mildred Middleditch sat stunned. She told her husband: "Mary was fucked by an angel." Gasp! "Dean Baines said so."

The Reverend laid a Baines Bomb at Auntie Joan's funeral. She was everybody's' aunt. A teddy bear of a person. Famous, she was, as a seamstress for the London stage. The curtain fell on that life, and then the play bill read 'Canadian War Bride'. People, even today, find it hard to believe she is gone. Most likely they are wearing clothes she sewed.

Droning on and on…

Wait.

Dean Baines is saying from the pulpit.

Auntie Joan was noted throughout the Kootenays for her rich and splendid garden I ask her once why her flaming gladiolas were so tall and straight and hard to the touch. And why as they reach their peak, there is such a burst of fiery blazing colour that seems to glow to extinction. Do you know what she told me? she said…

"Manure."

And at that very moment I thought about 'God'.

If you spread him around, things grow more beautifully you should spread him around your life too.

A pall bearer sitting next to me leaned toward me and whispered: "He just called God a pile of shit."

The Mystery of the Gypsy Tea Cup

I have known two gypsies in my wonder bread and mayonnaise life. They scare me. Still. Pablo who could talk to bears and Regretta who could heal home sick students by listening to the cards talk. Yes…you should be leery since gypsies have no home but the caravan and the road. They have wandered for centuries through Europe and Asia Minor usually as carnival performers. They are feared as thieves and a threat as thugs. Feared as purveyors of evil and worshipers of the devil. Hitler killed them nearly to extinction. But they are still here, and Hitler is not.

I also taught a Navaho student. Her special talent, really a gift, had an intimate understanding of horses and their moods, but this natural sensitivity could also communicate with other animals. She was held in high esteem by the town veterinarian. She was great with wolf wolves, but not so good with men wolves.

Everything about Pablo was huge. Beard, of course, streaked with grey. Voice, naturally, as if echoing from deep inside a well. Green tea eyes, yep, hypnotic. How old? Hard to say. Like a tree, you would have to cut it down to find out. The only extravagance were the rings on both hands. Ancient and ornate.

His family of gymnasts and weightlifters dates back some four hundred years. But even Pablo's bulk could not halt the gnaw of cancer. Pablo hadn't much time left to complete his opus on 'The Auras of Traveling Through Space'. He needed an editor. Would I? How could a clean shaven little old me refuse? And that is how the tea cup class exercise began. And the start of its curse.

Pablo was caught by the Gestapo stealing a leg of lamb from a German food truck to feed his starving family. Incarcerated. Pablo became so infected with lice that the guards feared a major infestation, so Pablo – lice and all – were hauled to a sheep farm on the French-Belgium border. They allowed him to sleep in the barn. Not much food, but he got all the harsh soap they demanded he use. The soap would probably kill Pablo before the lice.

Now, I'm just guessing, probably Pablo was somewhere in his early sixties when we knew him, and his skin was still scraped red and sometimes sore. And at times, some lice stragglers would appear. Some things in youth we never lose. Like, for Pablo, it was his odd sense of the ridiculous and a few hardy lice.

Within the year, Pablo fled to the French coast searching for a passage to England for himself and one harsh bar of soap. He found it.

The French are a sly and clever people. Duplicitous. The Germans are fussy and arrogant creatures. Officious. You take five French fishing vessels. You hide refuges in the hole of the vessels behind the latrine (Pablo and his soap). Three of the vessels over fish while two of the vessels rush to England with their catch of refuges. The three vessels share their extra catch, so they all appear to have fished together. The Germans never discovered the French ruse.

Pablo spent the rest of the war in Wales. He looked like a Welshman. After the war, Pablo earned a small fortune working in the oil fields of Saudi Arabia. He had no family. All of them shot when a German panzer division raided a gypsy circus. Just himself, now, searching for something in this world to adopt him. This yearning became his spiritual quest. The wandering gypsy. Pablo sought a place of spiritual solace. A well of restful zest. He traveled the world eager but always disappointed. Until…

…until he found the Kootenays and was somehow touched by the quiet sunlight and the silence of its earth. Here, he built his legacy: an ashram.

"You bury the dead, but you never bury their pain."

I am trying to remember his exact words, but it was cold on the hillside in front of the Ashram. Pablo was building a toboggan run for my kids.

"That's why Elephant Mountain appears to be sleeping. It holds all the pain of all the people who were drawn here. That's why your soul can find some peace in this valley. It is because of that rock outcropping where the eye of the elephant should be. And if you believe the eye is blind, you also can believe your secrets are safe within. Even when the Quasoonee lived here Elephant Mountain loomed over their camp sites, and now, it looms over a little town and all the lives that live there. Keeping the world out. If you want it too. Your choice. Always!"

Pablo is gone now. The lice finally got him. No! Stomach cancer. The ashram was kept alive until his fortune was spent by the last of his acolytes – Sarah. Pablo always had a woman by his side. The ashram was sold to the Anglican Church as a retreat house. The mostly deserted ashram was also found by hikers, raccoons, and grad ceremonies.

His opus was never published. As Pablo shrank smaller and thinner, his opus grew fatter and larger. Unintelligible to everyone but Pablo. I kept a copy hoping that time would clarify his spirituality. Until. One Christmas, in honour of our Pablo, we burnt his opus in a huge bonfire of dead sticks twigs and branches at the beach.

Few knew that it was Pablo who spent his fortune remembering the forgotten. Pablo commissioned a bronze statue to be sculpted to honour the many draft dodgers hiding from the Military and Vietnam here in the Kootenays. Many fugitive soldiers hid their wounds that would never heal even in the tranquility of these magic mountains. The statue was to be erected near the town's cenotaph where the world war one dead and missing were chiselled in the stone, until…

…until the VFW [Veterans of Foreign Wars] in Texas [the Dallas branch] warned the City Council. If the Council decided to honour these cowards and traitors, the VFW would boycott the Kootenays as a travel destination. The statue of the lone soldier was placed discretely in the town's cemetery as a grave marker for a helicopter pilot who committed suicide in his isolated cabin near Silverton. He wasn't found till the first thaw. His family did not want his body.

More anger is bred into the land that is the Kootenays. The government interned all Japanese and probably even those who looked Japanese in an encampment at Lemon Creek. They were oriental spies for the Japanese emperor. I wonder if the land remembers what has been done on it. The fences, the towers, the barracks are long gone. As if they were nothing more than nasty rumours. After the war, some Japanese stayed as a reminder, but most left. Returned to the city to begin again. They left some of their anger behind them but took more of their anger with them. Weeds can grow out of shit as well as blood. Pablo paid for the building of an historic marker at the mouth of Lemon Creek.

It was expensive. Very. It resisted being moved. It was like a shrine. It had been forgotten on a dead-end spur line in the rail yard at Desdemona. A lone boxcar rusted and rotting. All by itself. But if you look close enough, you will see cut into the metal sides of the boxcar the names of the Chinese who lived in the other abandoned boxcars in this shanty town.

These Chinese had sweated and bled, building thc transcontinental railroad, and died on those tracks that defied the mountains and rivers. And these Chinese were punished by those mountains and rivers. Disease killed them. Food killed them. Bosses' insolence killed them. And they killed each other drunk and gambling.

The pounding of the last spike in 1885, November of that year, and the transcontinental railroad, uniting the east with the west, was finished. The Chinese scum were paid their last pittance and abandoned, just more of the garbage and debris of construction. You won't find a single Chinese face in the famous photograph snapped at that moment in 1885 at Craigachie when the last spike was pounded into the ground.

Not a Chinese face anywhere to be seen. Their language and culture isolated them creating more hostility and indifference. They were hated because they weren't tall, weren't hairy, and yes, they were yellow and spoke an annoying language. So, they hid themselves and their misery and plight in shanty towns along the rail line they helped build. Until…

…until Sonwei (pronounced Sunway). Sonwei was hired to wash dishes in the kitchen of the Johnsonian Hotel. Promoted to prep chef. Then Assistant Chef. Sonwei soon moved out of Shanty Town to rent a room in a boarding house on Lake Street. Lake Street was populated by four bawdy establishments, three saloons, two boarding houses (meals included), and one lone church (Anglican). Secretly, the owner of the Johnsonian Hotel bribed the owner of the boarding house to rent to Sonwei. When they heard the rumour that a Chinaman had applied, two tenants had already moved out. (NO CHINESE APPLY HERE)

Sonwei ate all his meals in the kitchen of the hotel.

Sonwei was Shanty Town's hero. Now he would become their martyr.

Banks to Sonwei were crook infested institutions. So, he kept his earnings hidden underneath loose floor boards in his room. After almost two and a half years, Sonwei had accumulated quite a stash of cash. Down payment for his restaurant. Every night. The dream.

Sonwei was in the hotel kitchen when he heard the loud jangle of bells and the heavy hooves of the horses pulling the fire brigade wagon. He could smell the smoke from wood burning. Saw the yellow glow of flames. His Boarding House was a blaze. Frantic, he pushes through the bucket line of volunteers. Crazy chink! Rushes into the burning building. They found his charred body, and beneath his charred body, some coins and quite a bit of cash. The acrid smoke had asphyxiated him. The owner said Sonwei hadn't paid his month's rent. Looters scavenged the remains. Sonwei had no known family, other than Shanty Town. But Sonwei had started the migration to laundries, restaurants, and small groceries. Besides secluded gambling dens and opium hovels.

Pablo bought the boxcar and had it reassembled behind the ashram. On the boxcar door in large bright red Mandarin characters 'SON WEI' was printed.

PABLO SAID HE'D DO IT.

And the curse of the gypsy tea cup was just beginning. Students needed something to jolt their thinking. Students needed to always wonder what would happen next. A surprise. A shock. I was planning a class on the technical problems encountered in writing a paragraph about an incident. Hmm, an incident? Couldn't be violent, well, actually, it should be violent, but college students are notoriously physical. Who knows what would happen?

I had rejected a clown leaping into the classroom and squirting whip cream into the gaping mouths of students. The only clown I knew, since the theatre program was axed, worked at 7/11 and played kids birthday parties. Couldn't get off work. Not even for his vocation. He was sixty percent clown without his costume.

Like I said, Pablo said he would do it. I told Pablo to dress like people think Gypsies look like. Open slowly the classroom door. Don't say anything. Walk to the board and print in large block letters **'FREEDOM FOR THE GYPYSIES'.** Walk out of the classroom. Class, that was Pablo. But what did you see when you saw Pablo? Describe Pablo! Ten minutes later I had Pablo enter the classroom. I wanted the students to see how accurate they were in their observations. Since Pablo was there, I had him tell his story. The students loved Pablo. But I couldn't impose. I had too many classes. So, the surprise problem remained.

Pablo always had on his arm a lady follower. They would come and go, wander in and out of the ashram. Sarah would be the last. She would be with him as he passed through the portal of death and into the first chapter of his opus. Sarah loved Pablo and believed in his opus. When Pablo was gone, it was difficult to tell Sarah that his opus was unintelligible. For a while, Sarah was like a ghost roaming the empty Ashram. Then Sarah vanished and has remained vanished ever since. The forest is slowly reclaiming the ashram. The Anglican church seldom uses it as a retreat house. Hikers have no idea what the large faded red characters mean or what a boxcar is doing there without any tracks.

Pablo gave me a gift. A small treasure chest, the size of a bread box, that looked like it was stolen from a pirate ship owned by Long John Silver. And Pablo had just the idea for the treasure inside. And that's how I met the second gypsy in my life: Regretta.

A Regretta, in gypsy lingo, means, a sorceress! She was the last member of a notorious gypsy family to inherit the 'Gift'. For maybe three hundred some years, who really knows, The Regrettas told fortunes and held séances for a living. Her real name was Patricia Shinnick (Gaelic for fox). A spin of curious circumstance led her to our town and the opening of her thrift store 'Helping Hands'. Just about everybody has a similar story of not just passing through but 'finding' our town. But in the rear of the store was a very special room. The door was strings of gold beads and the walls were covered in red velvet hangings. In the center of the small room was a round oak table. On the table was a deck of spirit cards and a lit candle for each occupant in the room. Spooky, I suppose. But the perfect place to journey into the void of the occult.

Patricia became Patrick. Patrick Shinnick became a stowaway hidden by gypsy crew members on the freighter 'Lord Delaware' in route to Halifax. The gypsies and quite a few Irish (actually all of them) hated the English, and at least at the start of world war II, supported Hitler and the Nazis. Her family were extreme revolutionaries. They fully intended to blast a British Munitions depot, but the bomb exploded prematurely – killing her father, mother, and older brother. Patricia was hunted by the British for retribution. And that's why Patricia became Patrick who became Regretta, once the freighter docked in Halifax. Regretta? It wasn't long before she joined a gypsy travelling carnival as their fortune teller. And slowly jumped from town to town until…

…until the carnival played in our town, and like so many others before her, Regretta stayed behind, sensing the magic in the mountains of the Kootenays.

Patricia's long-time companion was Lily Rite, the Grande madame of the most popular bawdy house on Lake Street. 'LA BELLA DOUCHE' (The Beautiful Woman). No one would ever dare, at least to her face, criticize Lily's competence in French. Miss Lily Rite bought buckets and buckets of plastic lilies from the town's busy funeral parlour known by the yokels as the dead give away. There were vases of lilies that she doused with perfume all over the premises. Miss Lily Rite's establishment was popular – you bet it was. The mayor and the entire City Council except for one member with a vile case of flatulence were Lily's special guests.

When the silver king mine ran out of silver, mind you, it shut off the red lit lanterns of the Lake Street bawdy houses. Kaput those rip snorting, hell raising, bangabitch days, wilted even the plastic lilies. The new mayor Clarence Calhoun denounced Lake Street as a licentious avenue. He campaigned with a broom attached to his wheelchair. The crippled mayor was himself run out of office when he was caught masturbating in the council chambers over one of Lily's tantalizing pictograms. The town did its best to be quite respectable considering the moral decay of men and the sensual degeneracy of women. Lily Rite became Lillian Witherspoon, a righteous spinster who kept cats and bees. Something about that honey.

Lillian never accepted my invitation to speak to my class about those bygone days that were too hot to trout. Classrooms are sanitized chambers guarded by dutiful parents and school district boards. You should learn to read and to write and to arithmetic and nothing else. Not who you are nor how to live.

But Regretta always enjoyed talking to my class on the elements of time. She would demonstrate the art of fortune telling. A volunteer student would be selected. As a public reading, nothing embarrassing nor compromising would be discussed. I noticed Regretta was growing old and the demonstrations were exhausting her, so I suggested that we stop. Everything in its time.

Regretta will never be Patricia Shinnick to me. She will always be that mysterious soul of a fortune teller. The university attracted some students from Ontario and especially Quebec. Unbelievable skiing in the Kootenays. Powder waist deep. Every once in a while, I would notice a kid who exhibited signs of home sickness. It is considered a disease. And it can affect the most unlikely people – especially jocks. I have known students to return home after a week of classes. If I caught the symptoms early, I would call Regretta. I would then send the student packing to the Helping Hands thrift shop for rose hip tea and ginger snaps (the best in town). One visit with Regretta, and they were instantly cured. I don't know what she did. I was afraid to ask.

Regretta followed (almost) two rules. Number one rule: Never tell the fortune of family, friends, or lovers. Regretta told me once that the next few months would be difficult so stay calm. (The university shut its doors) But it will all turn out okay. (A sister institution hired me). Whenever we parted, Regretta would unnerve me by whispering "Behave yourself."

Rule number two: A professional fortune teller never tells the costumer anything about his death, even if the cards should show the end. The cards are a trick. They only help the fortune teller to focus her intuition and insight. You do not read the costumer's body. You read his aura. Regretta told me she only broke the rule once. Never ever again. And always regretted that once. The client, a middle age shoe salesman – obnoxious and belittling, angered Regretta who seldom gets sneered at. But it all depended on the shuffled deck of cards. The deck favoured Regretta's glee. The card it turned over was 'The ace of spades'.

That card suggests death is approaching. The ace of spades card was immediately followed by the king of spades. Preposterously unusual. Death of the client within six months. Regretta placed the two cards side by side in front of him, "You will die soon. I also see water." The shoe salesman was sweating and ashen. Trembling ever so slightly. He begged her to read the cards again. Obviously, Regretta refused. "What a fuckin' waste of money!" The salesman stomped out after deliberately knocking his candle to the floor. Regretta never saw him again, never heard anything about him. But she never forgot him. Regretta had committed a sin. Until…

…Until years later, just by chance, Regretta read his obituary the family had printed. The old copy of the Town Crier was a liner in an old chest of drawers she had bought. "Drowned in a sightseeing boat accident off the coast of Maui. They were watching whales."

Pablo and Regretta devised a hoax that would shock the students and test their skills of observation. Inside the treasure chest was placed an ornately hand decorated delicate teacup and saucer. Nestle them in a velvet cloth with gold ties. Regretta sells them for five dollars a set. She buys them from her supplier in Halifax for twenty-five cents a set. But tell the students that the saucer and teacup is your wife's family heirloom over one hundred and fifty years old. Tell the students to take a good look and describe the set in a paragraph. Set the teacup and saucer carefully on the edge of the desk. When you turn around, let your arm brush the teacup and saucer so they fall off the desk onto the cement floor shattering them into a million shards.

I did the teacup saucer exercise twice. Each time with the same result. The teacup and saucer did not shatter. They didn't even chip. They were indestructible. I felt like a fool. They sit to this day on a book shelf in my office. They have Gypsy magic so they will outlast the Earth. Some truth, huh, never trust a Gypsy.

I should have stuck with the clown.

The Tragic Fall of a Forestry Student

Do you ever think about the 'Beyond'? Not the near beyond. But the far beyond. It is my convoluted way of talking about death. Mine, primarily. Please… I want to die quick or crazy (crazy quick). 'He was run over by a wayward skate boarder whose britches fell down which flung his skateboard in the air like a javelin.' I don't want to linger. I don't want to have visitors with those forlorn expressions contritely ask, "How are you doing?" I'm dying that's what I am doing, you asshole.

I want to die like K. T. Weideman. Alone in his Cadillac! K.T. was worth eighteen million smackaoos when he went. That much could easily bribe both Saint Peter and the Holy Ghost. Mister Weideman had been broke three times in his little Lord Fauntleroy life. K.T. owed all his success to a twelve-book compendium 'The Triumph of the Will'. He loaned me, an eager teenager, the first volume. I got as far as the preface when I thought this is just plain stupid and went and masturbated. I did learn one thing. I would never be really rich or even rich enough if all I wanted to do was masturbate all the time. Anyway, who wants to be rich? Anyway, the government will fuck you over pretty good. Well, that's what the 'Triumph of the Will' said as far as I got.

If you stand at one end of K.T. Weideman's vast property, you cannot see the end of it. Nothing but grass and cattle. And below those hooves and roots: oil. Stick a toothpick in his soil and you have a gusher. K.T. was not extravagant nor was he parsimonious. His only luxury was the Cadillac he bought every September to drive around his land. No pickup truck for this country boy. The old beat-up cedillas were parked behind his ranch house. A living mausoleum of dead Cadillac.

The land, his land, is actually not prairie flat but hilly. Long ridges of hills thanks to bygone glaciers. The hilly rule being, honk as you reach a crest as a warning since you can't see until you reach the crest what is on the other side. K.T. surely honked, but the stray steer shitting a cow pie had no horn.

K.T. slammed on the brakes. The only alteration K.T. engineered was to remove all the headrests. They were useless. Uncomfortable. Wish he hadn't. A wrench lying on the back windowsill flew forward and broke his neck. His head was slammed forward against the horn. The blast of the horn frightened the steers away. The battery finally died as did K.T. Weideman in his cream silver Cadillac.

Unlike K.T.'s demise, my death will not be tragic, though it may have a touch of the absurd – and what doesn't. Like this – 65 million years ago some dinosaurs fell off the edge of the earth while the other dinosaurs became birds. That's why they are extinct today. Like that. My life – so far – has been one of many happy happenstances. I have always believed a clown has followed me around. Like...

I had just walked out of my office and stopped to talk to a janitor when a forestry student crashed through the ceiling onto my desk and chair. 214 pounds sprawled there. Ouch. What the fuck! The janitor immediately radioed for a clean crew and rushed in to see if the falling student hadn't been felled. Hey, everyone, I could have been squashed, so Ouch less. Cry baby!

Every April Fools Day, tradition has it that the forestry students pull a prank on one of their instructors. I taught forestry students technical writing. Last year, I was pranked. All my furniture was moved out of my office into the hallway as if the hallway was my office. But that was a minor inconvenience. My office was filled from floor to ceiling with giant red balloons. Besides students jumping into my office all day, they pop a lot. A lot!

The target this year was the land management instructor, Collin Hanes, who kept his office door locked all the time and his two daughters locked in a nunnery. Or so I have heard. He doesn't talk much (at least not to me). Why-I-have-an-office-since-I-am-in-the-woods-all-the-time-anyway office was next to mine, but on the other side of my office was the men's room. And that's where the forestry students found the entrance way to the crawl space above our offices.

The prank was quite simple. Super glue a whoopee cushion to his desk chair and then spread super glue on the whoopee cushion. One stuck woodsy instructor. Just try squeezing out of your pants when those pants are stuck... I kept offering my help... he didn't want any help... no luck in finding out at last if he wore bikini briefs... or so I've heard... called his wife who cut him out of his indignity. I am not saying anything. But... janitors have keys to all the offices.

About me and death and dying much too soon (do they mail pension checks to purgatory?), people can't believe how serious I actually am. And I guess that is sort of funny.

For Christ's Sake... Watch the Surfing Jesus

Everybody knows there is surf. Everybody at least has heard that Jesus could change water into wine. So why couldn't this fisher of men kick up a little surf in the dead sea. The God corporation parted the Red Sea, didn't they? You can't even mute the mute button so overwhelmed with the dexterity of my thinking.

I am just preparing you for the inevitable, especially if you are in need of a miracle or two. When the catholic university ceased and the secular university arose, the 'secularities' had all the religious icons banished from the campus. They forgot the wooden cross and the hanging metal crucified Jesus in seminar room 114. The crucifixion was so small that it hung insignificantly above the blackboards. Because of the octagonal tables, Room 114 was quite a unique seminar room. The tables' angles forced the students to react to one another. The yelling matches currently occurring in my Modern Drama class were between Paul Becker, resident atheist, and everyone else who had even a modicum belief in something.

The students that night in Room 114 were unaware of the history of the establishment they were inside yelling at each other. Except for the ideals of so many people and their ornery determination, the university would never have been built in the mountainous wilds of the Kootenays. It changed people's lives. Many people. I think that's why they saw them.

Usually on grey days or in the shadows of night. Always when the corridor was empty. She saw them. The art school secretary with her two corgis working on a cloudy Saturday afternoon. The chill started at the feet. The two Corgis were asleep when they jumped up, hackles raised, growling.

Two nuns. Hurrying down the hallway. They open the door to Room 114 and disappear inside. But classroom doors are always locked on weekends. Two tense dogs and a very scared art school secretary nervously checked. The door to Room 114 was open. They didn't enter. On the way back, they heard the door shut and lock. Others have reported when pressed at seeing two nuns. Never their faces. And never did the art school secretary work on Saturday.

I guess all I can say is some buildings are just brick and cement and plumbing, while other building people love having been in them. And these rare buildings absorb the spirit of these people, keeping their spirits alive until the building passes into rubble.

Paul Becker is there as is everyone else. All their hopes and dreams realized or abandoned. Held, kept in the lore of a building. A Bible if you will, of all the tiny miracles in life. Simply happenstance. But a building must have a memory – at least lasting a while in history. Like say a spectre. Then you have a ghost. Two nuns who will never leave MacGregor Hall. And those who from time to time will see them.

He will always be hanging there. The student who hung himself in the third-floor men's room. It was early spring, and the snow was still packed in the wells of trees. No chance – yet – for life this spring. Nor for him who hung himself. Him who I have forgotten his name. But MacGregor Hall remembers him. Some say they feel a slight chill when using that rest room. Others say they have heard footsteps traipsing down the third-floor corridor, but nobody was ever there.

Talbot Zubkoff has heard them. This modern historian has the office next to that men's room. It was Talbot's job to remember all the dates, names, places, and events most people forget or want to forget. Test him, Professor Zubkoff is infallible. Wherever he goes he is scribbling stuff in his notebook. Lots and Lots of 'Stuff'. No fun telling him a joke when he reacts – "That was funny."

Professor Zubkoff took it personally when a family of skunks burrowed under the library. And would not leave. No matter what the administration, obviously a bunch of stinking intellectuals, tried to do – including an exorcism. The skunks refused to leave. One of those wasn't-that-funny wits suggested that the skunks register for one of Talbot Zubkoff's classes. That would get those skunks to leave really quickly. But it was the students who solved the skunk invasion. They placed trays of uneaten cafeteria food under the library. And the skunks were gone – never to return.

Talbot Zubkoff has a thousand-word explanation for everything (including dates of course). Talbot did have trouble explaining the infestation of flies, then of course dead flies, that occurred every spring since the student hung himself. People would point to his office and say that was 'The Lord of the Flies' office.

Talbot was also flummoxed by 'The Portrait of the Smiling Jesus'. The controversy had happened before he arrived. And it galled Talbot that I saw the painting and he didn't. Couldn't.

No one knows who painted 'The Smiling Jesus'. It just suddenly appeared one day in the university chapel. And it immediately caused a campus controversy. The faithful believed he was smiling even in the pain and suffering of his torment. All had been sacrificed for his Father. His fulfillment bringeth the son peace. The not so faithful believed Christ was screaming out his despair. Hanging on the cross, suffering, near death, Christ realized there was no God. He had been a fool. The painting was an ink drawing. Harsh, hectic brush strokes. Deep dark circles under his shocked eyes. Then one day the painting of 'The Smiling Jesus' suddenly just disappeared. As if there had never been a smiling Jesus. It has never been seen since. I told Talbot the skunks took it and Mona Lisa is still smiling about it. Scribble, scribble, that was funny.

I was glad that Paul, even more our resolute atheist, didn't know anything about 'The Smiling Jesus'. Paul waited all term for Samuel Becket's 'Waiting For Godot', a godless universe of empty souls. Couldn't wait to be the boy who tells Vladimir and Estragon that Godot will not come today, maybe tomorrow. Gleeful, when in the second act, Pozzo is roped to Lucky, and Pozzo is now blind and lucky dumb. You can almost hear the applause in Paul's voice when our heroes say, "Let's go!" and don't move. Paralyzed.

Paul was being quite arrogant, badgering his riled classmates. He pounds the table with the clap of a judge's cavil. Just then we all heard a crack. A definite crack. We all turned toward the cross above the blackboards. The metal Jesus leaps from the wooden cross, flies through the air, hitting the linoleum, and, as if Jesus was surfing, scooted across the floor and bangs into the leg of Paul Becker's chair. Twirling as if in a whirlpool.

I get up and pick up the surfing Jesus and hand him to Paul. "You keep this in case you ever need a god."

Well, Old Man, What's Next? Bewixting the Young!

'Outrageous,' I acknowledge for those academics who were annoyed or especially irritated with me. I would naturally suggest 'Unique' or maybe 'Unusual', or even 'Unorthodox' which has a persecution ring to it. What cannot be debated is the slightly rushed quality to this book (as you have probably already noticed) Rushed because it has already been written. In memory! I am rushing to find the words to show those memories to others. Rushed? Rushed because Parkinson's decays the mind so the body slowly fails. I already feel my mind slowly slipping into silence. I figure I will live a long life, but it will not be me living it.

It requires five years to become a teacher. An agonizing internship. You quickly learn there are two clocks in any classroom. One clock tells you the time of day; the other clock tells you the age of the people in the room. So, you know what you can teach now and what you can never teach. The taxpayer hates a noisy classroom. But a silent classroom is a dead class room.

A teacher is not 'the' parent, but unfortunately is 'a' parent. So, teachers must build a fortress around themselves. To protect their own lives which are unfolding. There is a mob out there of pupils, parents, and public officials. They are carrying torches and pitch forks. So, no Socrates posters, please. It is always not so easy to hide behind your walls. It ain't Eden out there. Sometimes you have to teach the parent before you can teach the student.

You must continue to push, to challenge, to goad or you will become stagnant and feel useless. The first step toward burns out. The second step are some questions. Do you have enough energy to control the dynamics of a classroom? Do you have enough personality for people to listen to you? Do you have enough personality that you are willing to share some of it with others? There is a third clock in a classroom. Do you have enough time to do what you want to do? Can do? Just because the student fails, doesn't mean the teacher has failed. Sometimes, life fails!

This clock also tells you what is changing in society and what cannot change in the classroom. You know the truth but cannot always speak the truth. You are first and always a person. You are definitely not a saint. And certainly not a martyr.

Then after five years, you have the two most important questions to ask yourself. Am 'I' having any fun? Do 'I' have the magic to be a teacher? If you don't have the magic, you will just be a teacher, but not a very successful one.

As a young teacher, I was lucky to have a most unusual class. It lasted eight years. The enrolment was only women, usually from the age of 45 to 65 who loved novels. The morning moms. I loved Marcel Proust's 'The Remembrance of Things Past.' I don't know why. I didn't then, but I do now. It is very French the secret – a Madeline and herbal tea. I was too young, so the moms taught me. Proust's novel is so massive that we studied it for a full year. What a successful experience.

So, I decided to include Remembrance in my night 400 novel course. It was a disaster. We might as well have studied Proust's tome in French. What a Mistake! WHAT a MISTAKE! I forgot they were young. How could they possibly relate? And they never tasted a Madeline. And it didn't help bringing a batch to class. Yes, I was desperate. But out of this mistake occurred one of those incidents that I can't fully explain. And it all happened one evening, once again in Room 114.

But before we enter Room 114, I need to tell you about Maxwell Taylor. Max Taylor was a mining engineer, was, retired now, after travelling around and around the globe. He owned what he could stuff in his battered valise, but also stuffed in there was always a book. Max loves literature. He needed those stories. It got him out of his hotel room loneliness and downstairs to the hotel bar. When books began to bore him and he drank in his room, Max quit. He owned only the road. He owned nothing else. Not a soul. Other than the figure of loneliness in the bathroom mirror. Written on his fiftieth birthday cake was just MAX! Things were about to change. Boy, were they?

Maxwell Taylor married at fifty and was father of two children at fifty-five. By sixty, he had built his own house. Now, at seventy-four, he has arthritis, high blood pressure, and is fat – belly fat. Bored? Sure, now and then, but now and then he has someone to be bored with.

I first met Max after a speech I gave at the Rotary Luncheon. Often, he would stop on his way home on the North Shore. Talked mostly about literature, and the jungles he suffered. I had no jungles to offer but did have a literature class that term. A night novel class: Tuesday/Thursday, 7 to 9, in Room 114. He was welcomed to sit in any time. Yep, Room 114.

Jake Andrews was lambasting the choice of 'Remembrance of Things Past'. Condemnation after condemnation! "How do we know he knew anything about growing old? It's the turn of the century. What about us and his sentences are too long? I have plenty of questions the writer ignores with his melancholia." "Jake, I understand your frustration. What if I invited an old man to class would you listen to him?" Before Jake has a chance to answer, the door slides open. Everyone turns toward the door. Including me.

It was Maxwell Taylor. All of him. As if on cue. I hadn't seen him for over a month. Sick, I heard, with the flu. Everyone is aghast with surprise. Including me. I hang his coat on a chair and settle Max in a chair. I then turn toward Jake.

"Jake! You have some questions you want to ask Mr. Taylor?"

Jake Andrews firmly believes I had planned the whole situation. I would happily accept credit for it. But some things just happen. Or then again it could just have been Room 114.

Jake, this is for you. LATTER LADDER LATTER. "After a while, would you get me the ladder farthest from us?" Why students hate to learn English?

When I Come Home in a Limousine

Everybody stopped skiing on Red Mountain that afternoon. Everybody knew somebody on board Pacific Western commuter flight 1119 that crashed while landing in a snowstorm at Cranbrook. The 737 jet didn't know the snowplough would be on that runway; the snowplough thought flight 1119 had been delayed in Calgary. The pilot snapped his fingers pulling so strenuously on the stick. The jet would not climb fast enough. All perished…

…including Natalie Dejardin. She lost her chance – at least in this world – of ever finding her son, Jacob.

As I walked down the corridor to Room 114, I heard a ruckus. Loud for even this rambunctious first year composition class. Clapping. Laughter. I was horrified when I entered. There was Jacob. Naked. Standing on his head in the corner of the room. "Jacob get your clothes NOW! What's wrong with you people? Are you animals?" "He did it to himself." "You could have stopped him!"

"Pick up your things and get the hell outta here…"

I walked Jacob to my office. Called his mom. We all thought her schizophrenic son would be helped by the new medicine and being on a college campus like he should have been. From the start, I was worried. But I am always worrying. I get it from my mother. Good intentions, bad judgement. Jacob was a strong muscular dude. Anything could have happened. They had deliberately dared him.

I waited with Jacob on the front steps of MacGregor Hall for his mother to pick him up. The next morning when Natalie checked on Jacob, he was gone. And that began her torment of waiting. Wait-Wait-Wait. Waiting that's all Natalie could do after Jacob fled to somewhere, but no one knew where. No leads ever developed; no sighting ever appeared. It was as if Jacob had never been born. Never should have been born.

Suddenly, Natalie would stiffen in shock. Fearing what could be done to Jacob. He was a child, trusting and innocent. The days had some distractions except when a car pulled up front. Could it be Jacob? The window would reflect the lie she would always tell herself. The ghost of a woman went on as if her life was a play without dialogue. Everyone asked/no one knew. It was all because of the note he left.

The note Jacob left was held by his teddy bear that Aunt Rita had given him so many years ago. It was propped up against his bed pillows. The scribbled note read: "I'll come home, but when I do, it will be in a limousine."

That Wonderland Alice in a Penalty Box

I hate coaches. Some of them – NO – most of them. They are full of machismo testosterone, cliché ridden, possessed with stereotypes. They bagger berate curse condemn insult rant belittle, and any other synonym you want to add to that bloated sentence. Coaches turn babies into beasts and boys into warriors. Coaches gather the animals into a circle where they hoot and holler killer epitaphs at the opposing enemy team. Just like they did in Africa a million or so years ago. A coach would not be worthy of his jock strap unless all the opposing players were not stacked in an ambulance and driven to Emergency!

A Mayan coach had all the losing players beheaded. Some incentive. As the society decayed, the winning players were also beheaded as a gift to the gods (if you believe the National Geographic), It sounds more like the National Football League. I want one of these hot-tempered victory ballistic coaches stripped naked and his ass stuffed in a giant trophy cup. Then, paraded down Main Street (you won't find that in the National Geographic).

Sceptical, are you? Probably leery. SO WHAT! It didn't stop Dallas Taylor from sliding into my office. He moved like a hockey player even when he wasn't on the ice. Dallas was the star player and team captain of the Castlegar Gremlins. The final and deciding game of the tournament was that very night. Dallas said he missed class because he was at the hospital.

I had been slouching in my desk chair. It had been a long, long day. "Hospital," straightened me right away. Dallas knew I never took attendance. You come to class because you want too. It is my job to be interesting, even entertaining. Oh, good Lord, he wants to talk. So, I became really nosey, "So why the hospital?"

"The doctors found a small blood clot in my left leg." There is no such thing as a SMALL blood clot. "They are in the process of dissolving it." So why are you talking to me and not at home with your feet up? The coach suggested I do some mild callisthenics to prepare for the game tonight. "Who's your coach?" "Frank Waters." "Is this Waters guy a doctor?" "He manages the building supply depot." "What do your parents have to say about all this." "They are leaving it up to me." "What should I do?" "DO! There is no DO! There is one big fat fucking DON'T! You don't DO NOT take a chance of dying. If that clot gets loose, you will surely die or be paralyzed. All for one fucking game for the Castlegar Gnats. Gremlins. If you die, I hope they arrest the coach for attempted murder." The coach says that if I don't play, we don't have a chance at winning the trophy. The team needs me.

A few days after the tournament, Coach Frank Waters was interviewed in the Castlegar Gazette. "I was very proud of my boys. They fought real, real hard. They gave a hundred and ten percent. Now don't forget the memorial service for Dallas Taylor. It is being held at Saint Mark's Catholic Church 1190 Front Street at One pm Saturday March 27."

That last sentence about the memorial service could have happened, but it didn't happen. Dallas played. Dallas survived. Dallas won the game for his teammates.

The university hockey team, The Mountaineers, was also the town's team, unlike the pampered ego maniacs on the Canadian National ski team, Snow Gods. They dry land trained on campus. And attended classes on a whim, since they were too busy finding a cure for cancer. And by attending class they could belittle the other students into mediocrity.

Most of the Mountaineers' hockey players were on scholarships. They were hard working, conscientious, realistic students who respected education. Their coach, Pierre Rendue, was completing his bachelor's degree begun in Quebec. He taught them that to play hockey professionally was just a mirage. Use hockey to earn a university degree and possibly a career. You can still love hockey, still love that it is a team sport, fast, rough, and a ballet on ice. Pierre was, besides being very French, an earnest task master. Books first, hockey puck next.

Pierre makes my gaff even worse. I didn't know I was gaffing. Until the gaff happened. But a gaff is still a gaff. Begging gaff forgiveness is not happening.

The Gaff happened this way. The Mountaineers were scheduled to play the Inland Empire hockey team, The Ferrets, in Spokane, Washington on Sunday afternoon. It is at least a three-hour bus ride. The rivalry is thick. I scheduled an exam for Monday morning at ten o'clock. I wasn't told about the exam or forgot.

Will the writer please remember gaff forgiveness? The problem is not the exam itself, but the subject of the exam itself. Lewis Carol's 'Alice In Wonderland'.

Voila! Gaff! Coach Rendue insisted 'The' book be taken to Spokane, so the team could study on the bus. Unfortunately, the Ferrets (just like them) found out that the visitor's locker room was full of Alice In Wonderlands. Razzing and ridicule began as hospitality ended. Even the arena organist sang: "I'm late, I'm late/For a very important date/I have no time to sing or dance/I'm late, I'm late, I'm late." The game that afternoon between the Ferrets and the Mountaineers was recorded as the 'Alice' game. Never had there been nor since so many recorded penalty minutes and fights, NO, not fights. Brawls.

I couldn't believe what I was seeing. I had entered the classroom late. I had to pick up the exams from xerox. I set the exams on the front desk and glanced up. I couldn't believe what I was seeing.

It looked like the Emergency room at Kootenay Lake General Hospital. Black eyes, facial cuts and bruises, noses broken, teeth loosened, one arm in a sling. And stitches, stitches, everywhere. I should have assigned 'Crime And Punishment'. It is the only exam that I have ever invigilated where I had to administer blood transfusions and last rites.

I was afraid at any moment the players would break out in a chant. "Give me a 'G'. Give me an 'A'. Give me an 'F'. Give me another 'F'. That's 'GAFF!'."

With such turmoil and controversy, no one is quite sure what the final score was. The Mountaineers won – at least in Canada. And Alice wanders through the land promising never to follow a white rabbit down a rabbit hole. Especially if that rabbit hole is in western Canada.

Only Humpty Dumpty understands

There was one other class that was a horror to teach. It was a one o'clock Composition class where the majority of students were theatre majors. That morning a makeup artist had demonstrated some techniques. It is amazing what you can do with a little flour and water. The students decided to keep their zombie makeup on. Thank God it wasn't a Romantics class. After that my classes were known as 'Classes of the Living Dead.'

The Girl Who Was Eaten by a Crocodile

A magnificent mortal always angers the gods. So rare. So very rare. Thank the gods for that rarity, when out of the herd of humanity, the teacher should encounter a unique penetrating intellect or a charisma of sensual beauty. Teaching some 38 years, having taught over 7000 students, only 5 times has this brilliance occurred. 5 times too many.

The gods do not talk to teachers. The only hint we have to understand these mortals is to recognize the magic spirit they possess. This magic spirit may shelter them or ruin them in some mad careless escapade. A teacher burdened by a brilliant one is thankful for so many smart, gifted, intelligent ordinary souls. The calling of any teacher is to guide and nurture the gifts inside their students. And if a brilliant one should appear, like a meteor in a night sky, not to quake, since you are just a spectator to the ultimate game of fate.

When it happens… If you are a friend, be cautious. If you are a parent, be protective. If you are a teacher, pray. Disaster is always next. In brilliance, there is always a darkness. Those jealous, zealous gods manage the magnificent mortal's inevitable fate. Brilliance casts its own shadow.

Ron was born on another planet. Julia was born in a paint can that contained a coiled rainbow. But it is not where they were born or in what they were born that matters. What matters is how they behave within their destiny. Because the world is hostile to their brilliance – their intellect or their beauty or both.

Ron Statinger was intimidated by the bigness of a large university and by the vast biological organism of a metropolis. So, he chose a small university in the hinterland of Southern British Columbia. Ron traveled all the way from the Yukon to find in smallness the same elements as in largeness. He noted the irony.

Ron was tall and thin. Just skin and bones and a pair of glasses. But stretched over those tough bones was a covering of sinewy muscle. For as long as he could remember, Ron was a hunter's guide for rich Europeans or gangster Americans. They kill for a trophy to mount in their rumpus rooms. Ron was always amazed that at the last instant with the bear or elk in their sites the trigger finger would quiver, and the killer would hesitate. Often Ron would intervene. Ron killed with finesse. The bullet was shot into the brain of the beast, so the animal didn't know at what moment it was alive from the moment it died.

In early April, through late autumn, Ron would guide these scions of civilization. Ron sometimes wondered if these brutes had mounted in their rumpus rooms the heads of the people they killed through their passion or competition, jealousy or brutality. During all those short days of winter, Ron read books and educated himself. Up north, you do what you do; you don't what you don't. He was both student and teacher. That's why the classroom rankled him. He knew more than the teacher. Certainly, more than this teacher.

His world was a world of trees; the university world is a world of walking talking question marks and exclamation points. Ron was now unhappy in both worlds. In the forest, he thought of Herman Melville's ghostly white monster, while in the classroom he would hear the footsteps of the predator long before the animal smelled him. It was a mistake for Ron to come to college. Education for some is not a panacea but an exhortation.

Ron was an only child, though they had plenty of dogs in the house. They entered as puppies and left infirmed. His loving mother fed and bed him but did not understand him. Son and father were as one. Teacher by trade, outdoorsman by default. They didn't have to speak. They always knew what the other said inside their silence. One week before Ron was to leave for college, his father suddenly died of emphysema. When Ron had to finally leave, the dirt on his father's grave was not even dry yet.

Ron was (sort of) a student in my Modern Drama class. He defied me. Not in class. But on paper. After the class had studied a play, the student was required to submit a one-page long sheet essay. The theme was strictly up to the student. When I picked up Ron's submission, it was an illustration that revealed pictorially the essence of the play. I wrote "A+, Brilliant!" A class without words. What was happening to me? Where was the young teach who refused to receive a student's term paper because he missed by ten minutes the midnight deadline? So, my friend, pass by the past hurriedly.

The only exception to the one-page essay illustration was his submission for Ibsen's 'A Doll's House''. Ron's one-page illustration was an item in the

Personal Column in the local newspaper written by Nora Helmer. I can't remember what he had her say. I have kept no records except what I can remember. And that is grossly flawed. When you are young, you don't think you will even want to trace your footprints you left behind in that trek of beach you call your life.

Memory is an amazing amusement park. It keeps those terrifying embarrassing moments you wish it would conveniently forget. It stores some curious tinsel trivialities. Those quizzical, aborted lost moments, photographs remind us actually existed. But that amusement park in our head has forgotten them as if they had never happened. But how vivid what we old do remember. You can taste the memory. You can smell the memory. Even feel it.

I replied in the newspaper to Nora as her husband, Torvalds Helmer. I remember saying something to the effect that you are not wanted or needed. You never had children so don't ask about them. The actress who plays Nora Helmer has a horrible decision. The entire play rests on that decision. How does she leave her life? The play ends with Nora walking off the stage and out of her life (door slams, or shuts). Ron decided for his actress. Audiences have always wondered whatever happened to Nora. It was a play Ibsen never wrote or he never questioned the exit he never specified. "Brilliant!" "A+".

One of my students was a living Nora Helmer. She lost her children. Another of my students was a living Torvalds Helmer. He turned her children against her. He was Portuguese, she was Greek. They were a beautiful couple. I hadn't thought of them in years, until just a moment ago. Tomorrow, I will have once again forgotten who they were.

The final Modern Drama exam was too long and too involved. Another mistake. I might have written it with Ron in mind. Most students needed extra time to finish the exam. Ron submitted the exam within forty-five minutes. And to my amazement, his answers were carefully composed paragraphs with clarity and depth. The last page had the only figure. A chunky ornately costumed circus ring master holding a sign. The sign read: "SO LONG." This character appeared somewhere in every illustration that Ron submitted. I felt a vague unease. "Brilliant" "A+".

It was a warm, really hot, holocaust of an April. Most students had packed up and left the campus. Ron lingered. Worked part time with the landscaping crew. So, before he bussed North, I invited Ron to Sunday dinner. I could talk to

Ron like a father figure (I know what you are thinking). Enough, already. But you are right. I became instead the chunky little circus ring master figure. I knew something that Ron didn't know but surely suspected. His transcript. Grading in those days was accomplished with numbers not letters. I awarded Ron a 93 (A), but my mark was followed by four zeros – "0", "0". "0", "0" for his other courses. Ron Statinger would not be returning. He endured two years of being shackled to a pedestrian regime. What would happen to "Brilliant" "A+"?

I am the father of two daughters, but why not have a father/son talk with a surrogate son from another planet? I didn't know what I would say, but that had never stopped me in the past. Relax him. Let the tension ooze out.

As I turned the corner, the Ford Galaxy 500 (yes, the very one) was in car mileage: 180,000 years old. It always tugged to the right and listed slightly only slightly on turns. My second love was now cranky, obstreperous, and groaned a lot of chugs to get started. Refused to go over fifty. It would not make it through the next winter. It was destined, my second love, for the heap of all dead things. I hope it didn't hear me.

As I turned the corner, tilting nicely, there was Ron leaning casually against the civic center wall. But that is not really Ron casual. Benign indifference is more Ron casual. But inside that shy weariness was an electric engine that generated a hot-wired tension.

When I braked, you had to push down real, real hard, the headlights switched on and a strip of chrome flew off, just missing Ron. "Just throw it in the back seat. It does that all the time." While I was trying to switch the headlights off (pushing the windshield wiper button usually did the trick), I forgot to tell Ron not to slam the door shut. So, Ron jumped in and slammed the door shut. So naturally the window crashed down. The radio turned on. No one knows why, at least earthly ones, why the radio does not work during the winter months. I can understand that. And the ceiling collapsed onto Ron's little head. That's when Ron screamed. But that did shut the radio off. For how long… God only knows.

Obviously, Ron had never ridden in a Ford product. It doesn't help to talk about life and where you fit in the universe when you are shell shocked from having the ride from hell. Nothing memorable was said that evening. Nothing that Nora or Torvalds would consider significant. The evening was finished with the placing of the last piece of the Star Wars giant universe puzzle. Mostly black with a sprinkling of white star dots around one lone space craft.

I told Ron I would drive him home. He said, quite politely, that he would never get in that booby-trapped contraption again. He would rather hitchhike. And so, he disappeared into the night. We never saw him again. Never found out what happened to him. Just a people piece that can't be fitted into humanity's puzzle. I know readers do not like stories that do not have an end. That's memory for you!

Ron's life wandered from the North to the South for no particular reason but to see what was there. Julia Rosalie Cristina Cortez wandered from the South – from a little place (it just went by) outside of San Diego, Los Perdidos. Julia sought the Northern pale translucent sun light. Light that drains the neon out of a cascade of blues greens and browns. Tones, not splashes. Julia registered as an art student majoring in painting.

Julia and Ron attended the same Modern Drama course, but in different years. But both were drawn irresistibly to Ibsen's 'A Doll House'. To this very day, I can't even suggest a reason WHY? Why! Maybe because of the High School basketball coach who also taught me English. When we were studying 'A Doll House', he said Nora deserved what she got.

Oh, good God, not another Ron Statinger as I held Julia's first-class work sheet. There were dragons of every sort and size. All smiling with their very own ideas. Very few words of any consequence. Julia spoke in dragons. Unfortunately, I didn't. Beowulf or Mickey Mouse would have been better teachers for Julia. But I was her teacher. Critics, critics everywhere, but never an idea to spare.

But who is the hand behind all those smiling dragons? I learned more about Julia Cortez from her sister who came to retrieve her body. There were a few accidental meetings in my office and some insights from some of those dragons peering out from her writing. And then – of course – how could I forget the most unusual term paper I have ever received. I wrote on her title page "Brilliant" "A+". "Tell me, how can I help you?"

There are in this world two types of people: island people and continent people. Julia was an island person. Unless you could swim or owned a canoe, you couldn't reach her. Her very body distanced her. She owned a man's body – heavy shoulders, thick thighs, developed biceps. But inside, Julia was all estrogens with no testosterone to be found. You would have been surprised at the woman inside. Unloved. Many loved Julia – few, if any, she loved in return. To Julia, men were the list of ingredients on a bottle of baby aspirin. Women, on the other hand, were endlessly fascinating, possessing the very essence of creation itself. She only painted women and never in defeat. Resolute. Enduring.

Julia's long hair was black, heavy, straight, and coarse. Never a curl. A black hole would have been envious. Blackness caused by fire. When I first met Julia Cortez, I couldn't take my eyes off her eyes. So unusual. Julia possessed the eyes of a salmon madly fighting the rushing spring waters of a stream to reach a quiet lull to spawn and die. A life for a life. I still remember those eyes.

She painted – painted very few canvases. It was as if each painting extracted from her an energy spirit that could not be restored. A piece of her being departed with each work of art. There were very few paintings, but those few possessed luminous color with hallucinatory tension. Her paintings would leap from their canvases dominating all the other paintings hanging in the gallery. Her work had a lucid clarity as if seen beneath a veil of water. On a large canvas, Julia painted a huge orange – only an orange. It dominated the canvas. Her orange gleamed with the radiance of the sun. You wanted to touch it, smell it, taste it, devour it.

If intuition is so crucial to the effectiveness of a teacher, why hadn't I paid more attention when it rang. Maybe because I know in one of those ugly realities that intuition warns, but it does not – cannot – change what will happen. If that sounds like an apology, then it is an apology. So is this. I have other students, other obligations, family with their many faces. I am aging. I am not a monk. I am tired – very tired at times. And wish language wasn't so noisy. And that life wouldn't so often get tangled up with books.

When Julia actually attended class, she was always late, entering always with a theatrical flourish. But once in class, she always became that island with all sorts of dragons drawn on it. With each entrance, Julia wore a different elegant outfit. Obviously, her family was wealthy. I then noticed her outfits were not off the rack fashions but stage costumes – costumes from the Gilded Age.

Julia Rosalia Cristina Cortez was dressing as a female character from a play by Strindberg, or Chekov, or Ibsen. No matter what playwright you pick, their female characters were prisoners in a life they did not choose nor want for themselves. No death penalty. No escape other than senility or suicide. Intuition doesn't tell you the why of something, because sometimes it doesn't know why itself. A teacher is not one of the gods. A teacher has eyes, but no hands to halt or heal.

I bounced into the office. Plopped the banker's box of class materials on a chair. That's when I noticed it. Sitting… couldn't miss it… sitting in the very center of my desk. There sat Julia Cortez's term paper. Not a dragon in sight. I had told Julia how much my children loved her dragons. They were cute, even the evil ones were cute. They called her the dragon lady. I immediately flipped the thick term paper to the end to see how many pages. The assignment was one page. Pages: one hundred and twenty-four… You saw right. 124!

I became quite anxious when I read the title that leaped from the cover. 'On Becoming Nora Helmer'. NO 'On Becoming Nora Helmer'. YES. Later that evening, I opened Julia's term paper. And with dread, but anticipation, I began to read. By page 27, I was terrified. Julia Cortez was becoming Nora Helmer. By page 46, had become. Through the next forty pages, Julia/Nora wandered from sorrow to sorrow as regrets and prejudice and vilification ate away, like maggots, their wilful indulgence. Bitterness and scorn wailed from the pages. I feared the end.

Then suddenly the paper changed. It left any connection to reality. The paper had become fiction. Hopeless hope. Julia/Nora married a Swedish sea captain. They lived on an island. Since he was at sea most of the time, Julia/Nora would wander alone around and around the island. Remembering like wave after wave a life of so many regrets.

I didn't know what else to say. The final page was blank.

If I was an artist, I would have drawn a dragon crying. And next to the crying dragon, a dragon standing in front of a blank canvas with a raised paint brush. The third and final dragon would be a guffawing dragon. On the canvas is a guffawing dragon.

I sometimes bump into Julia in my memories. I then think about fate. Easy to do. Hanging in our house is a Julia Cortez painting. It reminds me of my inadequacies.

Behind them is a battered Ford pickup truck. In front of the pickup truck are two women trapped in the depths of the depression. Yellows, covered as if in dust, dominate even the black brush strokes that tell their stories. One woman is holding a baby. I swear the women are sort of smiling. I swear.

Her sister arrived to dispose of her possessions and to arrange the transfer of the corpse. I mentioned that she might read Julia's term paper to know her sister's struggles. I never mentioned the exam. In fact, I burnt the exam one night in our wood stove. She talked about how Julia, as a baby, couldn't wait to walk, and when she did, you couldn't stop her. She walked everywhere. Julia even found a way to climb out of her playpen. Wanderlust for sure. She never stayed very long in any one place. Her sister said, "I told Julia she would never find what she was hunting by wandering."

About six weeks later, a large box arrived from California. Inside was Julia's painting of the two women in the era of the depression.

Now about fate, unless you are a gambler you probably don't believe in fate. You don't understand fate unless you realize fate loves to play games. Why? Because fate always wins.

Final exams were written in blue booklets. Somewhere in that stack was Julia Cortez' Modern Drama exam. But where had fate placed it? I was at home at the kitchen table marking these exams. 1, 2, 3, 4, 5, 6, 7, 8, 9,10,11,12,13,14,15, 16. I pulled the next exam from the stack and noticed below it, Julia Cortez's exam. I set the fifteenth exam aside. On the cover of Julia's exam was a dragon waving good-bye. She had not signed her name to the booklet.

When I opened the exam, an ominous chill shook me. At the top of the page and to the far right is a little girl in a rose embroidered dress. She is holding a helium filled red balloon. To the far left is a crocodile. It is not sleeping. The text below is rambling and incoherent as if oblivious to the drawing above. Next page: The little girl and the crocodile are moving closer to the center. Next page: The little girl is facing the crocodile. Next page: The crocodile is eating the little girl. Next page: The little girl's legs are sticking out of the crocodile's jaws. The helium filled red balloon has floated to the very top of the page and is just about to disappear. The final page: The crocodile has swallowed the little girl and is staring straight at the reader.

I rush to the telephone.

The registrar gives me the address and phone number, but it is the California address and phone number. No local phone number nor address is listed.

I call California.

Her sister gives me Julia's address and phone number.

The coroner answers the phone.

Nineteen

I am not an honest person. Honestly, I'm not. Writing this memoir will certainly prove it to you. I would say in my defence that I am dishonest on special occasions ONLY rather than not honest at all. This is definitely a special occasion.

But… it is not my fault. You see… Memory is brain cinema. Memory is really little stories our brain tells us about our life, so we can live with ourselves, while we still have a self left to live.

If there was just one truth for each honest act, then I would not have to write that opening sentence. But there are many truths competing for the lead role. Like actors auditioning. And, of course, I am becoming increasing more senile – confusing things more than I like. Honestly! Come On! Who should care if this yammering is honest? Just so it passes the time, quickly, quickly in the late sunlight of an even later autumn afternoon. Here on the veranda. No one in my wheelchair but me. Pabulum and prune juice every morning promptly at 7:30.

Through one incident, I can remember my dad. All of him, all about him. In one moment of truth. Dad had sold his business and the family was moving to a new town. I would be enrolled in sixth grade. Dad, with my little sister in tow, were headed to the Shell station to pick up our car. I, as usual, ran ahead and was waiting for them in the office. When the gas station owner saw dad, he said to the mechanic standing next to him, "I hate to see him leave town. He is an honest man."

Dad had a very weak heart. That he lived so long is a testament to the man's love of living. I have not inherited his honesty nor his life love. My bags are packed, and I have bought a one-way ticket to Nothing Ville. No more of this life of pills and pain.

I looked out the bathroom window. There was dad. He was sitting on the guest house stoop feeding the chipmunks peanuts. And he was talking to them. He was old. How did that happen? As if overnight. That man had once owned two dealerships and now fed chipmunks peanuts. And talked to them. At thirty-three, I could not conceive what sixty-one would be like, other than being suddenly very old.

This summer, his last., was different. Dad didn't fish as much as usual. Fiddled with his air stream trailer. Played with his grand daughters and never drove with them in the car. He told me never to try to recapture the past (I didn't. The past captured me. When you are old, that's all you have is the past.). He spent this spring visiting old compatriots, but they had become grumpy, quarrelsome, and griped all the time. Dad finally found the house he was born in. Now just the foundations. Crumbling. The front steps lead to nowhere. A giant oak tree was growing out of the once sun patio.

Where's dad? We were chatting at the rear of the air stream. It was Labour Day. They were heading home after a summer of fishing and granddaughters. I was headed for the classroom. I went looking for dad. As I neared the corner of the air stream, there was dad, leaning over the propane tank, crying.

A curious letter arrived in early October inviting us for a family Christmas. The curiosity was its signature. Dad signed all previous correspondence with the business like 'Claude'. Never 'Dad'. He signed this letter "Love, Dad". I turned to my wife and said, "We should start preparing for a funeral". Two weeks later that phone call came.

I backed the red pinto station wagon (a tin can on wheels) out of the garage, so it would be easier to pack. I put the key into the ignition of the white Ford Galaxy 500 (a tank on wheels) to drive it into the garage. In many ways it was dad's car. He bought it for me. Best gift since my green Schwinn bicycle complete with fenders, head lamp, rear basket, jingle bell. I attached to the back wheel a playing card and a clothes pin. You could hear me a block away. The Ford Galaxy 500 wouldn't start. In fact, I never got it to start again.

Effie, Dad's mom. Lived longer than normal. She wouldn't miss her soap opera 'As The World Turns'. After each episode, the neighbourhood ladies would gather on the party line to haggle over that day's events. Usually concerning the antics of the villainess 'Lisa'. You could always tease Effie's ire by defending said culprit. In honour of Effie, we named our first born – 'Lisa'. From the grave, Effie's revenge was brutal. Lisa had colic for thirteen long, very long months.

Besides patience, you needed endurance to shop with Effie. She had to find out the life story of every sales-clerk. People would gush forth their most intimate secrets to the little old lady with the rich Texas accent and those tiny thick glasses.

Effie got ready for bed around nine, and by ten, she was ready for her nightly thick milkshake. Only vanilla. It helped her sleep. One evening, I told Mom who was busy darning socks, that I would fix Effie's milkshake. Into the blender I dumped vanilla ice cream, a tablespoon of vanilla extract, half and half, an egg. Then, I noticed a bottle of whiskey on the upper shelf of the cupboard. "Effie! How about a zing!" Effie was all for a zing. Into the blender, I poured a shot glass of whiskey. I thought she might sleep till noon or be discussing Saint Peter's life story at those pearly gates. Nope! Effie was up at seven thirty and unusually chipper.

The next night Mom said, "Time for your milkshake." "NO! No dear. Don't bother, Wendell will do it." By the time, Effie headed home to Texas, there was one empty Scotch bottle, one empty Bourbon bottle, and a half empty Rum bottle. Her very favourite. I slipped it into her suitcase. Me, the dishonest bartender to the elderly.

(Did you drink all that liqueur?
Nope!
YOU DID WHAT!)

I couldn't, I just couldn't tell the college community at the awards banquet why I admire this university. If I did speak the real reason, old noodle head would have had a conniption fit – and he and his noggin just inches away from retirement. The real reason why I admire this college must be hidden for a while – while I orate the public reason. It has nothing to do with honesty and has everything to do with 'not' being comic.

Stay small. I really do believe the larger the institution the less human it becomes. Large institutions have no time for individuality, no time for innovation, no time for humility. Ninety minutes into a three-hour exam that exam is stopped because the professor had to catch an international flight. A student working as a part time janitor finds the course term papers – unmarked – dumped in a trash cart. Feed back for five senior courses was eleven words. Most assignments and all exams are never returned to the student.

Being small on this planet is despicable, unless you are a virus. This could not happen at a large institution. It was terminal. Her stomach cancer. With the help of her friends, this single mom attended class. She loved the course and was determined to complete it. She was too sick to submit very much writing and could barely read the course texts. The registrar printed up on parchment paper a special award signed by myself, the Department Head, and the college president. We couldn't present the award in class. She had to be hospitalized. The award was presented in hospice care. She died ten days later.

The College is a grand place to shit. That is the real reason I admire this place. If you must know (and you must), I have always fought being constipated. Which, by the way, is a major symptom of Parkinson's. I would arrive early for my eight o'clock class. Walk briskly down the corridor. As I entered my office, I would hear my stomach growl, burble, and a bang bang of baby farts. Poop I would in stall two of the men's room right next door. I almost refused to retire. I just couldn't come to the college, shit, and leave. People would notice. Even if I brought my own toilet paper. Years of meta mucil now ahead of me.

Habit Ii KING! I felt comfortable in stall two. Stall two was an old and dear friend. I knew all the graffiti. The walls were cleaned, twice a year, of the students' angst and creative pornography. This ritualistic cleansing only encouraged the graffiti. Like ancient Rome's wall of curses. I felt hurt. Insulted. My name never appeared. Where had I gone wrong? Didn't I exist? Not a mention.

Then one day, 'it' happened. Recognition. I squatted down for some pomp heaven, and there above the toilet paper dispenser, in large black letters, were these words from James Joyce's 'Ulysses'. THE INELUCTABLE MODALITY OF THE VISIBLE. I taught 'Ulysses' in my novel course. The intellectual scrawl was better than a Ph.D. Although through Joyce, the student was saying, "See shit."

Professor of chemistry, Aldo Subatutu, was fleet of foot and entered – I must say – in a flurry the men's room. He lived life in a flurry. Aldo fled the local Togoland dictator with just his African robe on his back, but in the side-pocket was the family's secret hot sauce recipe. Aldo still wears his African robes as the last vestige of his heritage. Not to forget his family's notorious hot sauce. 'OHMESOSO' is green in all three flavours: hot, hotter, hottest. Hottest causes the smoke alarm to bellow. It does believe me. Aldo chose stall two (wouldn't you know it). I wanted to rip the door off stall two, but then Aldo might refuse to sell me some of his hot sauce. It makes oatmeal palatable.

I moped into stall one, then it happened. A rare natural event like an eclipse. ONE GIGANTIC PHHILARMONIC FART FROM DOCTOR ALDO SUBATUTU. The fart burst forth with a clash of cymbals. Roared with the roll of drums. Walloped with the yelling screech of violins taut strings. The walls shook with the blast of the brass. Students fled the bathroom in panic. It had to be the hot sauce.

I was staring at a cartoon of Professor A. Subatutu complete with his African regalia, squatting on a toilet while slurping from a bottle of his hot sauce. Birds and musical notes sprung from the toilet filling the air. The caption read: "I Can Out Beethoven, Beethoven!" Aldo's cartoon was just one of many cartoons where a select number of faculty members found themselves on a psychiatrist toilet. Talbot Zubkoff was sitting on opened history texts, so his dainty pink ass did not have to touch the germ laden toilet seat. One fly says to another fly: "At least history has a purpose!"

Except me. Neglect hurts. Wasn't my shit good enough. How constipated do you have to be? The students would prefer to fill my office from floor to ceiling with giant red balloons. Just try to get rid of them. They multiply when you are not looking. Even the day care center said enough already (I was mooned on the way home by a car load of beefy assed students. Life changing.).

Maintenance found the now notorious red striped notebook of toilet cartoons in 'The Pit' – the student lounge in MacGregor Hall. "A TERRORIST ATTACK!" so yelled the administration nervous over a cabal of art school students determined to seed culture on a vapid moneyed campus devoid of any life. The Baboon Brigade, by far the Brigade's greatest art attack was a giant block of cement buried in the ground next to the admin offices. Sticking out of the cement block were eighteen car bumpers. The chrome reflected the sunlight. Quite attractive, I thought. Of course, old noodle head and everyone else in the administration at least publicly thought it scandalous. Beethoven won't put bread and butter on the table. Probably old noodle head hadn't tasted Aldo's hot sauce.

The next night, The Baboon Brigade erected a giant green wooden letter 'F; in the gardens of MacGregor Hall. The night after that a giant yellow wooden letter 'U' appeared and it appears The Baboon Brigade loves to play scrabble. Extra security guards were hired. With guns too. The following night the letters '"C"' and '"K"' stood proudly upright in the parking lot of the Dog n' Suds. Eventually, and a short eventually it was, the four letters ended their spell check in the town dump. Spelled correctly – for a while.

For a man who loves the alphabet, I was sorry to see The Baboon Brigade vanish into history. Even Talbot Zubkoff didn't know who the rebels were. And I'm not telling.

The pounding grew louder. The stall two door was rattling. "Is that you in there, Wendel?" I must have fallen asleep. "I thought you were dead. Well, get out of there. I want to clean the place." I'd be the laughingstock if I died in here. Quite an arresting tombstone. You would finally make old noodle head happy.

The poundee was the janitor. A Lady. Lady Kiea. I nicknamed her 'The Goddess'. She was regal. A Cinderella janitor. Lady Kiea was raised in a military family stationed in countries all over the globe. Lady Kiea absorbed the culture of each country becoming more exotic with each posting.

It just happens, things do, you know, happen! The day of the stall two pounding was also the one-year anniversary of Lady Kiea's divorce. But since they were not officially married, it was one year to the day they knew they didn't love one another. Never had. How foolish they had been.

They owned perfect bodies. It happens. Even in an imperfect world. She, 'The Goddess', He, Grant Melnychuk, amateur boxer, owner of a popular boxing club. Trophies, trophies filled his cabinets. Grant left his testosterone in the ring. 'The Goddess' left her estragon to breeding wolf hounds. She once brought three of her pups to the college to show me. They were beautiful animals. Wild, yet docile to 'The Goddess'.

Lady Kiea and the boxer were bi-sexual. They intrigued people, so they had many liaisons. But they always came home. They loved to caress the curves and crests of their bodies' muscles. Hands brushing their taut skin as if their fingers were playing the strings of a harp. Each had a secret. Grant wanted a family; Kiea found a family abhorrent. And their secrets were their imperfection.

Gravity may rule the cosmos, but inside that huge glob of dark matter, at its very core, is imperfection. The universe is constantly breaking down. Forever falling apart. Harvesting life, seeding life. So, too, in the lives of people.

Lady Kiea had an abortion. She killed his child. She didn't tell him. He found out anyway.

Lady Kiea was standing in front of my desk, lamenting the last year. My desk looks out onto the hallway. My door is always open as far as it can. A file drawer blocks it. Next to the door is a floor to ceiling window. Plenty of light. Lamenting continues until we both hear footsteps slowly plodding down the hallway. Lamenting stops and Lady Kiea almost shouts! "It's the maintenance chief. I'm not supposed to be here. He can't find me." She quickly hides behind the door. Now, I'm lamenting.

My office has had its moments of notoriety. To the sinister delight of old noggin head. She wasn't even my student. She had failed a physics exam. Miserably. Her father was an evangelical preacher man. Full of stern Old Testament wrath. Buy that man a copy of the Kama sutra. She throws her physics text at my potted fern. Who is innocent in all this chaos? She slumps onto the floor in the back of my office. Refuses to leave. Ever. Don't physic instructors have offices? I've seen them. They do. If she leaves, I would buy her a plate of french fries smothered in thick grey gravy. A student favourite. NO! She plans on starving to death. How am I going to explain to the administration the skeleton in my office? I don't even teach anatomy.

Rescue arrives. A mature student in my morning composition class. He has three daughters. I have only two. I send him into the Lahr. I don't know what he does, but moments later out they come headed for french fries smothered in thick grey gravy. My potted fern still trembles at loud noises.

I know – I know – I shouldn't leave my office door open. (So instructed old noodle head) The college Trekkie Club chose my office as a meeting place. I guess the enterprise was somewhere in warp speed. I gather what happened is this. This: The office door was shut too firmly… a banished Klingon… he was seen urinating on a smiling poster of Captain Kirk… barged in to crash the meeting… who knows… maybe piss on a crew member… the door slammed shut with a whack… the Trekkie Club could not go where man had never been before… the jammed lock blocked them… even their Mr. Spock couldn't free them… the renegade Klingon roused the students in the pit to come and see the Trekkies in a Zoo!

Wouldn't you know old noodle head was a Trekkie fan. They still had to hire a locksmith to free the crew of the enterprise.

Footsteps plodding closer.

Keep going. Keep going. Lady Kiea is blowing kisses at me from behind the door.

Footsteps stop. It is not the feet of the maintenance chief. It is the feet of my neighbour. Collin Hanes. Good. Good! He never stops to chat. He is stopping.

He is turning toward my office. Oh Lord, no. NO! Collin is now standing in my doorway. "Do you have a moment? I have a confidential matter to discuss with you."

Lady Kiea is now miming speaking in tongues. ("I have a confidential matter, too. How about a woman hiding in my office?") Collin is now reaching for the doorknob. Oh, dear God, Collin wants to close the door. (What should I say? "Have you met Kiea? She is a very dedicated janitor. Gets every single dust bunny no matter where they are hiding.")

Collin grabs the doorknob and pulls but so is Lady Kiea pulling. "NOOOO!" I yell. "It's stuck. The door IS stuck. They are sending someone from maintenance. Faster than you think."

Lady Kiea pushes the door forward and steps out. Collin jumps, startled, nearly faints. Is absolutely flabbergasted.

"That should fix the door, Mr. Snark!"

"Thanks so much!"

Collin is in a daze as he steps back to let Lady Kiea exit said office. The expression on his face is the stunned look of a woodsman who has just seen a Sasquatch.

"Now what did you want to talk to me about?"

"I've heard rumours about your office. They're true They're true!" Collin Hanes wanders out of my office in a daze, shaking his head and fumbling with his keys. Hope the door opens – not all faculty members get such fast service from maintenance.

From down the hall, a voice yells, "Is there anybody in there?"

"Janitor!"

Twenty

He said, "I am Mr. Fuji Tamata." He was squat like a troll. He had large ears like a troll. He had a fat nose and puffy jowls like a troll. He lugged with him everywhere a large old-fashioned leather brief case unlike a troll.

I figured he was from Taddem – Taddem had a huge lead smelter and plenty of lead poisoning. Mr. Fuji Tamata said, "I am the Tamata from Taddem." I said, "What?" You see Mister Fuji Tamata had a soft voice like a ceiling fan that rotated only on very, very slow.

Mister Fuji Tamata opened his large brief case with some strenuous effort because of the thick lock and heavy straps. He pulled out of this leather chasm Playboy magazine after Playboy magazine. This was the subject of Mr. Fuji Tamata's term paper. It seems that their next-door neighbour has in his attic every Playboy magazine ever published. Mr. Fuji Tamata said, "It's a treasure trove."

If anyone in this world could find something boring about Playboy magazine, it would be Mr. Fuji Tamata. He went on and on and on as to what he wanted to accomplish. Even quoting from the stack of magazines. Maybe it was the rustling of pages and all that quickly passing flesh, but I became lost in a glorious reverie.

The next thing I remember is lifting my heavy head off my desk. I do not know how long I had been asleep. It could have been a year to a year and a half. I wanted to apologise but that would have interrupted his drone on his term paper.

I told the Department Head, leaving out the Playboy magazine stuff, what had happened. She said don't fret. It was the best sleep she had in a long time. Mr. Fuji Tamata was researching the haiku and his cousin next door collects Japanese trinkets. Talbot Zubkoff was also hit. This time it was the history of Kootenay lake stern wheelers. A neighbour has a garage full of books on stern wheelers. That is quite a neighbour and a fire hazard. "Do you think he is a witch?" "No! Definitely, a troll."

In the doorway, Mr. Fuji Tamata said that the committee had selected him to be in charge of the entertainment for the International Students Dinner. After his presentation, I am sure most of the committee members don't remember agreeing. Don't remember, period. What did I think about playing the national anthems of various countries? I asked if someone in the neighbourhood had a collection? No but his aunt did. Mr. Fuji Tamata had already recorded on his heavy reel to reel tape recorder you don't want to know. I heard myself saying that the playing of national anthems was quite appropriate. I just wanted to snuggle on a couch and snore.

The next victim was to have been the vice-president, who wanted to know what Mr. Fuji Tamata of Taddem had planned. I persuaded him that old noggin head was so very busy. Not to bother him. I know for a fact he loves national anthems. And he loves surprises.

My wife and I escaped during the playing of Bolivia's national anthem (the pre revolution one). You have heard it on Dole Pineapple Juice commercials. As anthem number eighty=seven played, Mr. Fuji Tamata sat alone by his tape recorder. All the other students had left. There were two faculty members asleep. Heads smashed on top of their dirty dinner plates. Old noggin head was snoring contentedly until he fell off his chair. The cleaning staff found him curled up under a table.

The next day a memorandum arrived from the vice-president. Next year, The International Students Dinner would be a picnic on Elephant Mountain.

Twenty-One

Jingle Jangle. Jingle Jangle. Jingle Jangle. It was definitely coming from the new men's restroom in the just dedicated 'DYNO HALL CREATIVE ARTS CENTRE'. I argued that you do not need creative (I lost); it was pretentious to spell 'Center' *centre* (I lost). The Dyno Athletic Attire Corporation built the new Center(re) because of their spokesperson, one Telley Anne Grafton – Darling of a nation, international skiing sensation, a chest full of gold medals, and a ski outfit full of loot. I am surprised she can still squeeze into the skin-tight Dyno Attire. Now, Telley Anne only races to the bank.

Telley Anne Grafton was an 'ex' student. Ex, 'ex', 'ex' student who studied few courses, attended fewer classes, and submitted fewest assignments. But that didn't stop the administration from un-closeting their academic garb to celebrate (their bounteous luck) their star pupil.

Telley Anne Grafton was peeved to furious when she discovered her name would not be highlighted on the building. To placate their smiling star, The Dyno Corporation named the elevator after her and her achievements. (a cure for cancer not among them) The Telley Anne Grafton Lift (lost that one too). Her portrait was attached to the back wall of the lift and her voice announced each floor – all three.

When the doors of the lift slid open onto the third floor, we were met with dead silence. The corridor was full of my English Composition students, first year psych majors, and an economics class. All on break. A path cleared immediately with bodies pressed up tightly against the walls. All conversation ceased abruptly.

I guess I should tell you who the other person standing next to me was! I followed the jingle jangle and the jingle jangle got louder as I opened the men's room door. There, standing by the row of sinks attaching the last bell to her left tit was a belly dancer. "I couldn't find the ladies' room." For some strange plumbing reason, the ladies' room was at the opposite end of this long corridor. (I don't know why they didn't call it the Telley Anne Grafton Ladies Toilet.)

"I can't find David Steeple either." David Steeple was the painting instructor famous for his ability to forget time and place and being. David's class was also on the third floor. I told her not to fret. I would gallantly lead her to his classroom. I would never pass up the chance to walk beside a real live belly dancer, since I don't ring when I walk. From the elevator/lift, we, mostly she, jingle-jangled as she pulled her wheeled suitcase full of her street clothes.

We jingled-jangled down the silent third floor corridor. You could hear every little bell tinkling. Psychology majors were especially attentive.

Then it happened…

Her wheeled suitcase bounced over a large foot that tipped her against a curly haired student whose curls tightened. And that, my friend, knocked that tiny little bell off her bulbous left breast and erect tit. For whom the bell tolls, I guess it tolled for curly hair. Curly hair picked the bell off the floor. "Curly, just attach it to my left tit!" As if Curly had done it a thousand times, the little golden bell snapped into place.

My students thought the belly dancer was headed for our class (For what academic reason, I could not imagine, although, I could try). They never forgave me. Our classroom was next door to the senior painting class. So, for the next hour, we could hear the faint jingling and jangling and imagine we were in some smoky dive in Istanbul.

The story of nude models or nearly nude models has another chapter to go. And it again concerns David Steeple. I should have learned. David naturally has an artistic mind. The artistic mind is not in time as somewhere in time. Remember now, it is a night class. It is a second-year composition class.

I was just ready to start when Dave stuck his head in. The rest of his body stayed out in the hall. I was afraid to ask why. Dave had hired a nude male model for his painting anatomy class. Any bells? No, no bells. The students need to be in a full circle. So, I switched to the smaller classroom. Dave promised to tape a note on the door announcing the classroom switch. Three aviation students were always fifteen minutes late because of a flight simulator scheduling conflict. Surprise, surprise, Dave forgot. I didn't know aviation students could blush.

Aviation students are the most macho of all the college students. They eat machismo for breakfast. And actually, they believe they fly the plane. They make forestry students look like sissies.

The three aviation students bound into class as they usually do. Grab the first empty desk. Grab a pen and their notebook. Ready to write tonight's complex sentence. That's when they start looking around. They are not in Kansas any longer. That's when they see the naked nude model sitting on a podium. That's when they recognize their physical education gym instructor. All of him. And more, much, much more. Each aviation student put down his penis, oops sorry, pen.

They know, as everyone knows, you can become homosexual with just a flick of a pen, oops sorry, penis. And you know the rumours about coaches and gym instructors. I AM NOT GAY! Keep repeating, so you don't have to wear a pink tutu in a gay parade. David rushes three freaked aviation students out of his class and dumps them at my door.

"There's a naked man next door!" They keep repeating, hoping the image will go away. They swear he waved at them without raising a hand. The rest of the students look at them as if they are queer or at least nuts. The three aviation students are relieved I didn't have them describe their naked gym instructor, although the next gym class was to say the least – awkward.

Twenty-Two

The alarm clock rings…and the day begins. NO. Life begins. You drive to work – there are challenges and routines – you drive home to dinner and family – and set the alarm for tomorrow's life. No story here. Just lots and lots of glorious life. If you want a story, you have to read a novel, watch TV, or just plain gossip.

Soap opera characters are very sad because they never have time to live their lives. Since they are daily bombarded with story after story, they have infidelities and weddings like a handful of M & M's. Jack be nimble, Jack be quick, Jack just jumped some sweet chick. (For the seventeenth time)

Jesus' life, as a rogue preacher who angered both the Roman magistrate and the Jewish hierarchy, died nailed to the cross on Good Friday. But on Easter Sunday, with the stone rolled back from the tomb and Jesus walking around quite alive, the life of Jesus Christ had become a story. Twelve men (one a traitor, another a coward) would take the story of Jesus and turn it into the richest religion the world has ever known. How? Why? Well, Christianity incorporates being born again into its lore. And that idea is irresistible.

But how to teach the difference between a life and a story? And how easy it is to become a character in someone else's story.

In the middle of the classroom, I place my daughter's doll house. Sitting on the roof is a Ken doll and next to the Ken doll is a Barbie doll. They live in a perfect world on perfect world street. The doll house is empty, empty because they don't actually have a life yet.

Soon each member of the class will become a character in their story. Once inside Ken and Barbie's story, the students will be forced to make decisions – and experience the agony of deciding. One scenario reads this way.

It's August, and graduation from high school seems years ago. Barbie intends to join the business administration program. Ken has received a scholarship for engineering. He is a wiz at math. In June, on graduation night, having drunk too much, Ken and Barbie make love in the back seat of Ken's father's Lexus. Now the students, one by one, get involved. I choose a student. "You are Barbie's best friend. She tells you she is pregnant. What would you tell Barbie?" And so, the story grows. Barbie wants an abortion. Ken wants the child. All sorts of characters are created.

The class is over, and I am in my office when the irony occurs. Shortly I will become a character in some one's story. He is standing in my doorway. "Do you have a minute?" I have come to dread those words.

Is a teacher bound by the confidentiality that binds a lawyer or a priest? Yes! It is assumed. You don't have to sign a document. Telling his story to some friends over coffee is one thing, writing the story in a book is quite another. I have no plea or no excuse. I am a story addict. And this story is pure heroin. I am betting that time, over fifty years, has washed away the events and its people as it does to all our petty endeavours.

I can do this much. He will tell his story as far as I can remember him telling it.

"My brother is three years older than I am. He is the handsome one. Even his brawn is handsome. A Hollywood swash buckling hero. Casanova with sperm in bulk. I got the brains, poor eyesight, and a lousy thyroid. Girls love my brother. He creates dreams for them that you would find only in Harlequin novels. Girls always ask me how I am doing.

One girl was so obsessed with him that she literally fell down seven flights of stairs and bounced twice. She was determined to marry him. She usually, No, always got what she wanted. She was the only daughter of the owner of the building supply company – Kootenay Homes. She was not a princess. She was a queen. But I must say a very beautiful and quite generous queen. Much loved by her court. Her girl friends told her not to marry him. He was too wild. If you want a trophy, yes, if you want a husband, no. Little good if any would come from this relationship.

Over the last three years, we have become very close. I am the only one she invites to her anniversary meal. I think some how she sees in me – him! She told me her girl friends can't possibly understand since they had never felt what I have felt. The softness of his lips. The tensile strength of his biceps. Or his tight thighs like coiled rope. The hot surge of his sticky semen. The gasps. The groans. The depletion. Both bodies trembling. Then like fire the orgasms would blaze again. Even years later, thinking about him, she would experience his hot surge.

After a night of boozing, my brother woke up – engaged. Her parents bought her an exquisite engagement ring. The wedding rings would out flash it. As the rings would out flash this spectacular wedding. Like something from a glossy wedding magazine. He wasn't consulted on any of the many plans. He didn't care to be. I don't think he believed he was actually the groom. I was amazed when he chose me as his best man. And the queen was pleased too. I would have to take extra thyroid medicine.

The strippers were maudlin. He played along well. He was indeed the recipient of all the worship. If she was the queen, he was the would be king. They were destined to reign. Those glossy wedding magazines again.

At the rehearsal dinner, for the first time, I noticed how quiet he had become. As if he was asleep, and when he woke, he would be somewhere else. Instead of sleeping in their new condo, he drove home with me. Mom and Dad were asleep upstairs. We were in the living room drinking beer. He was. Booze effects my thyroid medicine. That's when he blurted it out – "I don't love her. I don't love anybody yet. She is just another rich bitch. I don't want to become his son. I don't want to manage a building supply empire. No wedding. I am not getting married. I am leaving town, tonight. I am going back north. Where I belong."

I didn't argue with my brother. Never could. In our few physical altercations, he never ever hit me. Just held me until I calmed down. I said: "No, you're not." I said: "You are not letting her dress in her wedding gown tomorrow morning." I said: "You are going up to her house, tonight, now, and tell her the wedding is off." I said: "And then get the hell out of here. You know you can't live here any longer."

My brother drove out of the drive in the rain. More a mist. He should have taken his motorcycle. He didn't. He took his Jeep. It was passed midnight. It was almost two. He was drunk – breathalyser drunk. I still feel bumps of guilt. I know I couldn't have stopped him any way. Even with a gun. Two guns and a rifle.

The queen's family live in Crest Haven. It is a steep climb to get there with many sharp curves. On one of those curves, the Jeep slid on the wet pavement. The next morning, they found his Jeep in a ravine. His neck was broken. The newspaper photograph of the twisted Jeep would not appear on a glossy wedding magazine.

The wedding had become a funeral. The bride, a widow.

After a year, the queen was still grieving. She lived in their condo. She no longer pursued her nursing career. And she refused all dates, even the most innocent.

Most people, no, everyone stopped trying to break that grief that consumed her life. I stopped on the second anniversary of his death. She showed me in her bedroom an altar she had designed with large photographs of my brother and some of his belongings. A couple of letters he had written when he bivouacs in the Yukon. And two large candles that she lights every night. She is still obsessed and will always be obsessed. It is hopeless. I fear at night she may on occasion wear the wedding dress I saw in her closet when she yanked a sweater from a hanger.

I had fully intended on telling her why my brother was driving up to her house at two in the morning. He didn't love her. She should stop wasting her life on a false love. Two more anniversaries have passed and each time I don't have the guts to tell her the truth."

"Do you love her?"

"Of course, not."

"Yes."

"I guess I do."

"Then tell her now! Now! She probably won't believe you. She will probably hate you. Obsession only grows stronger the longer it is left to live. Tell her. Tell her her grief is a lie. A lie is eating away at her life. What choice do you have? Nothing else has worked."

A week or so later, he stopped by the office. I had another minute. He couldn't do it. He couldn't tell her. Maybe the truth is worse than the lie. One thing for sure. This is one story that I don't want to be a part of.

Would you?

Would you tell her?

Twenty-Three

At 4:37 PDT, the ordeal began. It was a Tuesday in late September. I had an evening class – seven to nine. I have forgotten the exact date and have no recollection of the year, which is crucial because of what I want to tell you. It concerns a gray metal wastepaper basket. Such an incidental object to appear in a tragedy. But it has become just one of the many nightmares that flash in my mind, especially at night. They are unforgiving. I should have been a plumber.

The incident must have occurred in the late nineteen seventies. That would make me 36 or 37. Still a young teacher. This piece jumps around a lot. Sometimes I'm 52, sometimes, I'm even 80. There is one other clock. It is ticking throughout the entire piece. It is inevitable. It cannot be stopped. You can't see it. But you can hear it as if someone is breathing. It reads seven o'clock; it stops ticking at 7:06. I guess, because I am preaching, I need all these clocks. Only old teachers should be allowed to instruct. Not because they are necessarily wiser, but because they have learned the difference between being smart and being stupid. They have looked into that gray metal wastepaper basket.

At 4:37 PDT, it happens. Death. That death, the one I never cared to learn about because I was too busy playing with life. Like comedy. It is easier. Death, like tragedy, is harder. A lot harder. You want a reason for death and the universe is not reasonable. And the reasons you pose are so specious or downright ridiculous you find yourself becoming cynical without realizing it.

At 4:37 PDT, an old man, somewhere in his late eighties, has a heart attack and dies instantly. His Chevrolet Impala crosses the double yellow lines slamming into a Ford Fair Lane killing the driver (my student) and severely injuring his passenger (she was also my student). Death seemed ludicrous in the fiery yellow sunlight of a molten blue sky with most trees by the side of the road in oriental dress. The world dies in autumn, not students. It must have been awkward, the old man and the young student, standing next to each other at those pearly gates waiting for Saint Peter who is just as surprised as they are.

At 5:22 PDT, a student calls. He tells me about the accident. He asks if there will be class tonight? Without really thinking, I say "Certainly!" "Now if you can't make it. I understand." In my pride, I was saying NO to death – death would not stop my class from happening. Now, an alien invasion from Mars is another matter. But if just one student shows up, I would have to say something. I have nothing to say. Except, right now, there are probably Martians living in the Kootenays.

At 5:48 PDT, I was – still – just staring at a stack of papers sitting on my desk. I was staring at death. I started to shuffle through the work sheets. I had planned to return them that evening. This moment in time… this very moment in time… this always moment in time… my mind will forever remember. There are quite a few 'whys' in that last sentence. The sunlight had gone. And for the first time I realized how gray my office was. As if the gray had washed all the colors away. Even the metal wastepaper basket was gray. But it wasn't gray. It was a dark, dark green. Now, it was gray.

At 5:49 PDT, I found his two assignments. For a moment only, I considered recording the marks in my grade book. How foolish of me. It didn't matter. I laughed. It really didn't matter. So, what matters? Really? Nothing matters, I guess. I intended on asking him to register for a lower-level English class. Both of his assignments had failing marks. The writing was listless even in its superficialities. So, unlike the real him – a box of Chinese fire crackers. Such energy, much enthusiasm. He had the physique of a football player, but he couldn't lift a book. I dropped the two assignments into the wastepaper basket. They fluttered slowly down into the darkness of the wastepaper basket. Disappearing into its endless depths. It echoed the darkest of all thoughts. I found her assignments. Top marks. It didn't matter either. It doesn't matter whether she survives the wreck and lives to be a hundred. It will never matter. Of course, it's existence. A drab vacant theatre whose stage is empty except for a hanging light bulb, a tall step ladder, and a gray wastepaper basket. I pitched her papers into the trash.

At 5:53 PDT, my fifty-three-year-old self is sitting on the couch watching my thirty-six-year-old self hunched over his anxiety. I am just an image, an image of a 53-yearold. I know what to say to this grieving class, but of course the 36-year-old teacher can't hear me. And the gray metal wastepaper basket is sitting right beside his desk. The young teacher is alone in his time.

I also see my eighty-year-old Parkinson's self in the bottom of that wastepaper basket. I remember wanting to take all the papers of all the students and spilling them into the metal gray basket. All of them having lived their lives, and now, eighty, like me, they are decrepit, having squandered all the beauty of their youth just to survive. Having found their success, having found their evil, now, just wadded up paper lives waiting for death to cart them off to a dump. A gray metal wastepaper basket.

At 6:17 PDT, his dilemma has become a quandary. Cliches, every idea became a cliché. He couldn't, although he should, clear his desk and place the grey metal wastepaper basket right in the very center. Then, take the marked papers and throw them into the wastepaper basket. "That's what we are confronting tonight. Any night. Every night." "So, what are we going to do about it?" They were too young for such a reality. I am too old for such a reality.

Funny! I have always found funerals funny. And difficult for me to maintain a grave demeanour. "Two Presbyterian ministers are sitting in a large black cannibal pot, cooking. One minister says to the other minister, 'Do you think they will say grace?' 'The cannibals chief sends his oldest son to Oxford. Upon the son's return, he tells his father that eating people is wrong, except for Catholics. But you can't eat them on Fridays.' He couldn't remember any jokes. Anyway, it is probably macabre. Macabre because of what he believes at eighty."

Thirty-six does remember Pierre Eddgeton's funeral. Pierre, Professor Eddgeton, taught French with a heavy Scottish accent probably caused by his club foot. He loved France but was squishy passionate over French cuisine. He was two thirds Camembert and one third Brie. Pierre love jokes. The dirtier the better. That's what I loved about him. He had almost as many jokes in him as cheese. His autopsy must have gone ha-ha squish squish.

That's why I nearly stood up at Pierre's funeral mass and yelled at old noodle head who was giving the eulogy. The same eulogy that he gives at every funeral. The same eulogy he probably gave at his son's hamster funeral. HYPOCRITE! ALL OF YOU ARE HYPOCRITES! Not once did he mention Pierre's love of jokes nor give some examples. Life had killed, or at least cheese, Pierre – and now the church had murdered the identity of Pierre's self.

The funny is out. Definitely. Gather the few students who actually attend around a table and just let them talk. Maybe in their words they will find the student who died and the one fighting to live.

At 6:38 PDT, my 80-year-old self was sitting next to my 53-year-old self on our 36-year-old couch in his office just a few minutes before he had to face a most unique and frightening class. A class he would ironically forget happened in the busy years ahead. And not remember until his own death is eminent. We could have told him what he would learn in the years ahead except for the corridor of time and all its locked doors. This is what we would have said.

Inside the darkness hides the light. The darkness is serene and beautiful. It fathered the light. Before things were, the forces of the dark shrank to such an intensity that the dark exploded releasing the children of the light. Space now became known as the dark and time became known as the light. This is when a God was created – created by the union of the dark and the light to tell all the creatures about the relentless enmity between the light and the dark. That the dark gave birth to the light and the light will eventually die in the dark. The dark waits, becoming stronger. The more the light creates the weaker its time becomes.

God is a ruined paradise. His two attempts failed. He created the angels of light and they rebelled and were punished in the dark. Then he created humans who also rebelled and were punished to struggle and suffer in the darkness of earth. God now sells from civilization to civilization worlds wide this gimmick called: A heaven.

And the why of our who is never explained nor really ever confirmed. Although homo sapiens was given a wish-it-was-a-bigger brain so we can pretend to find our way somewhere to ultimate bliss. Many of us play the Parker brothers board game 'Christianity'. We roll the dice and move through the spaces of childhood, youth, adulthood, and the elderly, waiting to reach heaven. We gain as many Faith cards as possible against landing on those Despair cards. If we reach the last space (The Reality of Heaven), we have actually reached the first space (The Promise of Heaven). In its darkness, our Faith cards tell us what we have found. But players, a warning. If your despair cards ever out number your faith cards, you lose and must begin your quest again.

Remember players. Evil does not exist outside of your brain. The brain is our God. Its quest, like God, is to fuse the light and dark in a place of harmony. When the brain malfunctions, it creates evil. All of life is the illusion of this miraculous yet imperfect evolving brain. So, Death becomes your only reality. It leads you to and then through the portal to the next.

Wish I could tell 36 this. The very sensitive instruments of astronomers let them listen to the rumble of the explosion that created the cosmos. This rumble emanates from the very edge of the expanding universe. There as everywhere else the dark and light are in continual strife. The rumble sounds very much like laughter. The light and dark are ridiculing their gods' pathetic efforts to sell a sham Heaven. And what should we ask our neighbourhood God about this heavenly fraud. How about. Is God laughing 'WITH' us or is God laughing 'AT' us?

I wanted to help my 36-year-old self. That's me at 53. Confident and contented. Ironically, I never had an opportunity to use the Game of Christianity. It was too convoluted. When a student was troubled with someone close dying, he certainly did not need the esoteric. At 80, I don't believe in all that previous shit spouted by 53. If anything, I believe in the grand nothingness. Peace. That's all. Peace. I don't want another human soul; I don't even want a golden spiritual soul. Just. Quiet, please. Eternal quiet.

At 6:50 PDT, a 36-year-old teacher had slowly gathered up his material and left his office. We watched him go. And were frustrated that he couldn't know what would happen to a member of their carpool just a few calendars ahead. The carpool consisted of an English teacher, an art historian, a psychologist, and a philosopher, Harold Coates, who taught a popular course on Death and Dying.

During a rather warm early Easter Holiday, with the snow soft and deep in the high meadows, the philosopher's youngest daughter was caught in an avalanche, buried, and suffocated.

I had admired my wife's two-layer dark chocolate cake, as our friend, Tony, just did. My wife had frosted the cake with creamy white frosting. It was a gift to take to the memorial. I thought the cake needed something extra. Too plain. I found this little plastic doll that was in a container of cake decorations. I took the doll and stuffed her head into the white frosting so just her little legs stuck out. There I dare you to give the cake to Professor and Mrs. Coates. We burst out laughing. And burst. And burst. We would stop and then it would start all over again. The audacity of giving that cake to the parents of their child killed in an avalanche started the laughing all over again. We got control. Finally. Then my wife said: "Do you think the white frosting is too much?"

We were surprised that Harold didn't speak at the memorial. We were also surprised that he didn't finish his courses. And further surprised when he retired from teaching. He never taught again. Never road with the carpool. Occasionally, I would bump into him. He was pleasant but withdrawn. He had spent many months in Africa with his missionary daughter. Supposedly, healing. Harold bought a skiff and sailed every chance he got. Supposedly, healing. The members of the old carpool were horrified. If our philosopher could not handle the loss of his beloved daughter, what chance had we mortals.

The Gods were not finished with tormenting the philosophy professor who dared to understand their nature. Harold suffered a sudden and massive heart attack. The days that followed, Harold became intolerably constipated. A huge bowl of bran topped with prunes didn't help at all. So, they gave him a powerful laxative. A gigantic fart trigged a heart attack and that's what killed him. I told my wife not to bake a two-layer dark chocolate cake with white icing. She said, "How about a prune danish?"

At 6:58 PDT, the 36-year-old teacher was slumbering down the dark corridor toward room 114. The slower, the longer. He heard the faint murmur of voices. Not the normal bang bang ruckus. Behind him, following in the shadows, were his future selves 53 and 80. They wished that their 36-year-old self could have seen in the middle of his panic how easy and natural it would all come out later on.

36 would be sitting in his office, eating Skittles. I heard what happened. I am so sorry.

(She is an accounting major, he is into biology. The wedding was set for Queen Victoria Weekend. Easter Holidays were spent on the island at Pacific Quest Beach. They stayed an extra day. She was packing their gear; he had crawled up on this rock out cropping to snap some shots of Pantorum Misantus (A West Coast moss). Suddenly, without warning, a giant wave roared in. When the wave withdrew, he was gone. They never found him. Not even his camera. It was as if the ocean had eaten him.)

The rush of grief. It unnerves folks. You think you passed those emotions when, bang, the sorrow hits you. They're called the sixes – six minutes, six hours, six months, six years. But grief can't possess you or you will never be free to have your own life.

(She is dressed in a simple black dress and a scarf in shades of lavender. The only other adornment is a gold pin shaped as a leaf. She is frightened. She wakes in the middle of the night and he is standing at the foot of her bed just staring at her.)

Don't be afraid. What you are experiencing is quite normal. You are slowly saying goodbye. These apparitions will become quite rare very quickly. Some people tell you to get rid of all his things. Nonsense. He is a part of your life. He will always be a part of your old life. But it doesn't mean you can't find a new life.

In some strange way I am envious of you. Of your opportunity. You have lost a whole world. You need to find a new world. You will have to journey and discover the world again. You will have to define everything with new eyes. You will see things you never noticed before. You are exploring everything new. It will be difficult for a while, sure, but when the ordeal is over, you will have become a better, stronger, more sensitive, more aware individual. Don't lose him to grief. Don't lose your self to sorrow. Explore. Adventure.

At 7:01 PDT, our young teacher enters the classroom. He stumbles. The classroom is packed. Students not registered in the course are sitting there. No one is saying anything. They are all just staring at the young teacher. You could tell some had been crying. I placed the stack of work sheets at the edge of the teacher's desk. I noticed beside the desk was a gray metal wastepaper basket.

At 7:06 PDT, I caught myself just staring at them. In an extra loud voice to hide my nervousness, I said: "Take out a work sheet and turn to page 78 in your Grammar Gym. This evening we are going to study the crazy world of punctuation. Invented by a bunch of crazy monks transcribing the Bible in the Medieval World. And Laurel and Hardy are going to help us understand how to use these crazy signs."

You could almost hear the entire class sigh their relief.

Life must continue as long as it can. Whether it ought to or not is not our question. Ignorant at 36. Ignored at 53. Despair at 80.

Twenty-Four

The Gods are watching, even the children of the land, especially the children of the land. These children heard about the pristine paradise of the Kootenays, where condoms grew on trees and those exotics sounding sexual ills had not been born yet. They would find solace in these mountain valleys. They would find peace in themselves and in their communes with the far east sounding names. Many others before the children sought dreams of finding gold and silver and even religious freedom. But…

But… Paradise is tissue paper in the wind. Even the lush years of the fruit orchards ended in the blight. In fact, all those other wayfarers had their dreams end in blight. Kootenay is Indian for 'the valley of lost souls'. A quiet place where dreams come to die. For some, when the dream ended, they woke to the consequence of having experienced something sad and beautiful.

They called themselves 'Hippies'. Flower power children. The world had suddenly become young. Their religion was their music and the world was their enemy. They would last maybe a decade. Then, they disappeared. Grew up, I guess. Or they angered the gods and the gods punished them with their own ideals.

They fled Los Angeles. They fled Montreal. They fled Toronto. They were fleeing Mommy and Daddy's middle class two car garage materialism. They fled ugly mundane farting reality in a stew of drugs that could out race time itself. Could paint pretty little pictures and call them truth. They fled war. They fled the hypocrisy of religion. They even fled each other. But could they flee the disease that infected society and would cause each one of them, one by one, to succumb.

I let my hair grow long. I wore psychedelic clothes. I taught 'Jonathon Livingston Sea Gull' (to my eternal shame). One morning while shaving, I looked out our bathroom window. I saw a guy on a unicycle wearing a tuxedo and a top hat bicycling down the highway. And thought nothing strange about it.

I will always remember that one winter night. It was rare that I lost my temper. Boy, did I ever. I was teaching a second-year literature class that traced the history of tragedy from Greece through the twentieth century. I loved that course. The class was mostly hippies and they didn't believe tragedy even existed.

It was a Myth. A joke. A cheap Hollywood horror show. The class leader was their hero. The very symbol of the hippie dream. I can't believe I have forgotten his name. So, how about 'Todd Van Hemert? Todd was born to a wealthy Dutch family from Montreal. He was tall, muscular, with a mane of hair so blonde it was really white. No scars. No blemishes. No scratches. No pimples. As if the world was not allowed to touch him.

Todd was always ten minutes late. No offense intended. Todd was ten minutes late for everything. His two older brothers, who were also in class and just as blonde, said Todd was late being born, so was always trying to catch time. I thought it was those heavy hiking boots he always wore that slowed him down. We could always hear his heavy hiking boots clopping down the hallway. Then, we could start class.

So, Todd said: "Oedipus should never have fucked an older woman." He said: "If Oedipus had loved less himself and more others, he would have avoided road rage." He said: "It isn't love that is rotten in Denmark." He said: "Let love replace avarice. Let love replace revenge. Let love replace pride. Let love replace skulduggery. Even let love replace the often gibberish ridicule of comedy." And then Todd said: "Only Yorick has love and he jesters the court from the grave."

That did it! I had had had, had it! These stupid silly superficial idealists. Let nature speak. Stop life, go love. Yes, love can save a person, but love cannot save the people of the world. If anything, did love prevent the extinction of the dinosaurs. Our extinction. Listen to nature. Love is the beauty that becomes the flower's death trap. The spider loves her beautiful web. Poison is her elixir.

I am warning each and every one of you. Do not anger the gods with your foolish ideas. Do not transgress their rule or they will surely punish you. And the punishment will be sudden and severe.

They looked at me as if I was a raving nut. Raving yes, nut no. Driving home I realized I had become a character in a play. I had become a Casandra. I feared, like Casandra, would I tell the future but not be able to change its course. I wondered. If Shakespeare were alive today, would he write a tragedy titled: Todd Van Hemert.

That was January, now it is July. Coming up the drive is Todd Van Hemert on horseback. He had not ridden out of a Hollywood western flick. No cowboy hat, but a white Yankee baseball cap. No chaps, but Levi's. A Kokane beer tee shirt. What no cowboy boots, no spurs? No. Those damn heavy hiking boots. He stopped to find out what course I was teaching in the fall term. When I mentioned I was thinking of a sabbatical, Todd's reaction was curious. "No! You were born a teacher. There is nothing you can do about it. You are one of the most successful teachers I know. You are never smarter than your students. You think with us."

"I will teach if you promise to be on time."

"I have a gift for you." I wish in hindsight I hadn't done this. "I want you to stand under our Yew Tree. It may be 400 years old. The Indians believe if you stand under a Yew Tree, you will have eternal youth." Todd Van Hemert did. And the myth worked.

That was July, it is now late August. From across the lake, if you look for the nose of Elephant Mountain, you would have seen their large bonfire and hear their bongos playing. What you couldn't see or hear was the strong current that sweeps by the Elephant's nose, as Kootenay lake narrows into the Kootenay river. And the river rushes on to the dams.

It was an odd night. Still. Quiet. The moon was just a sliver on its way to being full. A cloudless night. Warm, warm for this close to September. And September's chill was ready. It would soon make a memory of summer's heat. And there was nothing anybody could do about it.

The clan had been hiking all day. A couple of kids were snoozing against a bright green canoe beached near the bonfire. Beer cans were scattered everywhere like a battlefield of dead soldiers. The smell of drugs wafted in the air to the pleasure of dizzy mosquitoes.

Someone yelled, "Let's Go Canoeing!" The canoe was shoved in the water and kids jumped in a hodgepodge of bodies. Already the current was sweeping them along. Someone up front shifted their weight and the canoe flipped pitching the kids into the cold water.

The current grabbed the canoe and swept it away. Some instantly swam to shore. Todd could only dog paddle, so his friends held him up as they fought the current to reach the shore. As his heavy hiking boots weighed him down, his friends, one by one, had to leave him. They were sinking. He was pulling them under. Soon he was left alone to drown.

Not a scratch. Not a scar. Not a blemish. His grey body lay naked on the West Lake Hospital autopsy table. A picture of eternal youth.

His mother riding the angry bull of grief screamed hysterically as she beat and slapped the body of her son who would now be always late. Yelling, yelling, yelling, endlessly yelling curses at her other two sons for letting Todd die.

I stood behind the lectern in the sanctuary of the Cathedral of Mary Immaculate. There was no casket. No urn. The body was shipped back to Montreal for burial in the family plot. Against the wishes of his brothers. They had no money for a lawyer. It was handled secretly. Too late to stop them. I placed on the lectern three crumpled sheets of the clan's eulogy to their Todd. No one in the clan felt they could read it without being overwhelmed with sorrow. So, they asked me.

To the right of me at the lectern was the family: dad, mom, sister, grand parents, aunts, uncles, cousins, business associates. The men were dressed in blue suits, mostly. The women, of course, were dressed in black. To the left of me, dressed in garish, neon lit, psychedelic attire as if an explosion had occurred in a paint store, sat Todd's two brothers, the clan, friends. Down the main aisle flowed a river of hatred and vile resentment. The commune was not invited to the reception after the service, so my wife invited them to our house to celebrate the life of Todd Van Hemert.

August had become September and September would become October, and in November, I would learn how wrong I had been about something I thought so right. I wanted them to grow up, and when they did suddenly grow up, I was horrified. They had registered for my novel class. They were mature, serious, perceptive, conscientious. Their youth had been amputated from their soul, when youth should fade like summer flowers. The exuberance of youth should be enjoyed as long as possible. Not exorcised.

They had brought flats of food and cases of beer. I was watching them from our veranda frolicking at our beach. Laughing. Splashing. Running the length of our boat dock next to our tilting pink boat house (we couldn't afford a boat) and leaping into the water. You could easily spot the blonde hair of Todd's brothers. Shafts of sunlight slanted across the beach as the September sun slid behind Elephant Mountain to shine in another roost of the world. For now, for the moment, the last of the halcyon days shone brightly.

They left their sorrow with us
And their lice

Twenty-Five

And I had to cheat! What's wrong with me? And of all places, 'The Mini College; Where? Where regular morning classes are cancelled so staff and faculty can attend a whole menu of presentations. A noon lunch is thrown in to keep the herd happy. It was old noodle head's joy and pride galore. My talk explored how images reveal character. I finished my demonstration around 11:45. I heard a couple of stomachs growling.

I was gathering my paraphernalia and stuffing the stuff into my banker's box when I noticed two bright yellow index cards on a rear desk. They said, "Would you like to comment on the quality of the presentation?" Presenter: __________________. Topic: ________________. Miffed. At least annoyed. Two folks in my talk didn't even bother to comment. I didn't even know we had comment cards. Well, shit on them. Them of course being old noodle head. Sounds like him.

I'll comment on my own talk. On one card I wrote "Wendell Snark could make the telephone book interesting." On the second card, I was just getting into the mood. "Professor Snark is the finest teacher in the Kootenays." 'World!' seemed a bit too much.

I was late. I threw the last tidbits of stuff in my banker's box and trotted out of the classroom. Completing forgetting the two comment cards I had left on a rear desk. I remembered two weeks later. WHEN! When the monthly college newsletter arrived in my mail box.

Old noodle head is of course editor-in-chief. He printed my comments. I should have used 'World'.

Twenty-Six

'The Day Before Never' rhapsody

The overture

A diamond necklace in a ditch melody… A brown notebook of scribbled poems melody… A kiss of warm air on the forehead of an old man melody… A pair of down hill skis discarded at the starting gate melody… Refrigerator magnets strewn across the kitchen floor melody… A bedroom full of trophies melody… An old sagging couch slip covered in bright shiny marigolds on a pearl blue background melody…

The libretto

A mother is biologically bound to her new-born son. The father's role has his sperm penetrate, and once his sperm has dumped its load in the egg, his job is complete before anything is actually created. She of our ancient heritage is to 'care'. He is to 'dare' the competition with strength to kill for shelter and eats.

The iPhone era has confused the roles of the prehistoric family. Mothers today are becoming fathers and fathers are becoming mothers. One psychological phenomenon remains. In the song created between father and son, there reaches a crescendo where the father knows that if it came to a fight, the son would win. The son knows that his fresh body would beat the stale worn body of the father. In a frightening moment, the son has become the father and the father has become the son. In the music between them, strength is the arbitrator, respect the judgement.

I know a father who would arm wrestle with his son on every birthday. The deal When the son beats the father, the son no longer has to obey the father. Both father and son were in my class, when the son finally beat the father. No, no defeat, Triumph biologically, since over the years they had forge a love between themselves. Their melody was played by many different instruments in their orchestra. Sperm had nothing to do with it.

Some fathers should never have been fathers. Had no idea how to be a father. How to care? How to understand? How to sacrifice? Some fathers even deny they gave someone life. By hiding. By running away. By neglect.

How many sons have gone searching for their fathers and have been rebuffed? The door to the father's new life slammed in their face. So, they leave searching, now, for a substitute dad. Some fathers eat their sons. Rapacious. Jealous. Cruel. Brutal. Don't know the difference between a hug and a choke hold. Do not know when to lose at arm wrestling. Do not understand when the needs of the son become greater than the needs of the father.

It all depends on the song that plays between them. Their very own melody. Played the last time when the father is buried by the son.

A diamond necklace in a ditch melody

You are listening to the cry of the son just after being born. You cannot hear the cry of the father. He has fled. But every year the son receives a birthday card with a fifty-dollar bill inside. Never a return address for the father.

On the son's eighteenth birthday, the father suddenly appears at their door. All apologies and good wishes that sounded loud in the silence. The father is not invited in. The gift he bought for his son is inside a long narrow box. An authentic copy of a samurai sword. The plastic handle is painted in dark wood colors.

The son wants to register as a fine-arts major. Although surprised, the father offers the son a couple of thousand dollars for tuition. They plan to meet next Saturday night at the junction. Ten o'clock. Sharp! The father is driving through on business.

The son almost left. Almost left. Almost left. Almost… the father pulls up to where the son is standing. Over an hour late. The father rolls the window down but doesn't turn the engine off nor does he turn down the radio. "Glad you waited." Regrets. He doesn't have the two thousand. Maybe in January. "You understand how it is. Your old man had to buy his new gal a gift. She better like it. The diamond necklace cost your old man eighteen hundred bucks."

From the passenger seat, the father picks up a velvet box and slides it through the open window. Click the lid lifts. A diamond necklaces. The son grabs the diamond necklace and tosses it into the ditch beside the turn off. The father flings open the door to his sports car. The father's fist misses. But the son's fist cracks open the father's nose. Jabs a fist into his father's mouth splitting his lip. The son's foot slams into the father's gut, knocking him into the ditch. The son climbs on his bike and peddles into the night. His tee shirt wet with the splatter of his father's blood. Minutes later a sport's car speeds by. Its angry horn blasting the night away.

A brown notebook of scribbled poems melody

I am busy sorting through papers packing my banker's box with the gimmicks of that class. When I noticed him in the back of the empty classroom. He was fiddling with a brown notebook. I heard the organ of the hockey arena and the crackle of the public address system. I wondered if we all create a music that would surround us. Obviously, beside the bulk, he was a hockey player. My music would be a lounge piano – don't forget the empty brandy glass for tips.

He was asking me as he was handing me the brown notebook. His hand was trembling and his voice – shaking. The empty classroom seemed to amplify the sounds. "Would you have some time to read a few of the poems I've written?" (I tried not to look surprised) "Sure!" (I was surprised) and you wouldn't be.

A week or so later, I asked him to stay after class. I was very impressed with his poetry. I circled some techniques that show just how advanced his symbolism. I am always amazed at the maturity of young people. I told him he should continue to explore his talent.

"I don't think so."

"Why not?"

"I'm just a dumb hockey player."

"Who told you that?"

"My father!"

The fire alarm bell blared in my head. I seldom, if ever, win a battle with a father. They are impregnable. Infallible. To break free of a father's biological and psychological strangulation requires will power. A father who does not know his son will eventually lose that son.

I knew if I hired one hundred cheering critics yelling "You're not dumb… You're not dumb… You're not dumb," the father's one word dumb would brand the son as you would a steer.

A kiss of warm air on an old man's forehead melody

When you hear the father enter, hear a military marching band. The family called him 'little Hitler' whispered behind his back. He hated any back-yak. They agreed their only victory would be to outlive him. And they did.

They dumped his ashes at midnight on a pig farm just off Hadley Road near the falls. The ashes probably turned the pigs nasty. The father was a vile, vindictive, vicious man.

On the way home from working at the smelter, he would buy a Hershey bar. Then the father would line up his three children in front of him. Two daughters and a son. "Now who should I give this candy bar too?" No one dared speak. He would never choose the son. He later in life ate much too much. His favourite daughter was always chosen. She was forced to eat the entire Hershey bar in front of her brother and sister.

With his pants yanked down to his ankles, the son was routinely beaten in the barn with a mule strap. For the slightest infraction. Some imagined. When the father got too old to beat them, he would tongue lash them. All three of them left home – early. The mother was left to serve him as many spoiled meals as she could get a way with. She so wanted the clock to fall off the wall and kill him.

When the father became more senile than sinister, the son found ways to taunt him. The son bought a large orange couch in Portland. He threw the cushions in the back of the Volkswagen van and roped the orange couch to the roof of the van. The border guard asked if he had anything to declare. He answered "No." "What about that orange couch on the top of your van?" "What orange couch?" The border guard let him pass. And the father hated every minute he was forced to sit on its orange-ness.

The father was dying now. Just days, maybe even hours left. The family rejoiced smelling the brimstone of hell's fire. Not a single member of the entire family ever went to see him drift toward the fog of death and the retribution of God's judgement. Except one. Once only on the very day he died.

The son.

The son told me he didn't know why exactly. It wasn't to gloat. It wasn't to guffaw. He felt little real sorrow for the old man. A sorrow tainted with the bile from a lifetime of hate. A sorrow that had not a writ of forgiveness in it. There was nothing to revenge. Like all of us eventually, death will steal everything we have ever owned. Life meets death, nothing meets nothingness.

A couple of times the father's hand reached out, but the son pretended not to notice. And the hand fell back onto the clean white sheets. The father asked for one last favour. He had beaten the son to make him strong – to survive the treachery of the world. He loved his boy. Would he kiss him goodbye?

The son was disgusted. Nauseated. He should never have come. But he bent down leaning over his father's forehead. Closer, nearer. The warmth of his breath brushed against the skin of the dying father. The father sighed a smile.

"But I never kissed him. NEVER, NEVER, NEVER"

The father died silently later that afternoon.

A pair of downhill skis discarded at the starting gate

The part of the son is sung by Mickey McQuire. The chorus is sung by the Ski Officials of the Magic Mountain Ski Resort. Mickey is waiting in starting gate two for the buzzer to send him down the course which would be his final run – more ways than one. Mickey is a natural born skier unlike his brother. The part of the older brother is sung by Danny McQuire. Danny was a fierce ski competitor, but never could win. Danny had no style, but plenty of strength, where as Mickey had all style but little endurance. Danny would lumber down the slope while Mickey danced.

Mickey was so far ahead of the pack of the Magic Mountain Invitational Downhill Tournament that all he had to do was coast down the course to win. Mickey wanted to quit skiing. Last spring, he had told his father. The part of the father is sung by Maxwell McQuire. Mickey told his father he wanted to quit. His father was furious. "You are not quitting, not with your talent." It didn't come to blows, but almost. Just threats. Mickey wished he had his brother's strength if not his support. Maxwell wouldn't talk to Mickey for weeks.

Right now, the father is at the bottom of the hill adjusting the video camera. He is singing his son's praises to a local sports reporter. The video camera would record the standard two fists raised to the sky salute. Maxwell could hardly wait for the Wednesday edition of the Mountain View News and the typical photograph of Mickey McQuire holding his trophy, sometimes Maxwell was included.

His father wanted all his trophies displayed on the mantel piece, but Mickey was insistent: NO! The trophies were kept in a trunk in the cellar. Danny was jealous enough. There were snide comments and a couple of friendly brotherly wrestling matches turned out to be not so friendly.

Mickey had no choice. He knew he had no choice. Attending college this last year, he had heard other music. He didn't know what this music meant yet. But he knew he couldn't listen to the small-town orchestra. It had nothing to do with love, but everything to do with boredom. His escape would happen, even if it meant the pain of an injury. Mickey was desperate. He was certain about this. His father would be beyond fury.

The buzzer flipped the gate open and the clock began to count the seconds. Mickey McQuire just stood there. Then he stepped back. Took off his skis. And walked away.

Refrigerator magnets strewn across the kitchen floor

Johnny Dubrowski. Say it out loud. Sing it. Listen to a language that you don't know the meaning of its words and you are listening to the music that language creates. When a people die, the music of their language has died before them. Without their music, they could not hear their heartbeat. Some people speak their essence in prose while other people sing, sing a poetry that is a passion. Johnny Dubrowski.

Jon-knee-due-brow-ski… I remember a paragraph he submitted where he described some items in an antique store window. The description was raw and vibrant. The style was slick and scintillating. Just like Johnny. Johnny was my daughter's middle school volleyball coach. She had a crush on him – as did most of the girls. Those Caribbean pale blue eyes and that deeply rooted charm. A very unique person with a special writing style. I swear all I wrote on his paper was "Stupendous description. What style! You should do something with it." I swear that was it. Johnny Dubrowski…

Johnny Dubrowski just that fast zoomed into my office and slapped the paper on my desk. "How did you know I'm gay?" "I didn't, I just thought you were a fine writer." "Does the clique know?" "NO!" The spaces indicate the awkward pauses. I should never have used 'Stupendous'.

Johnny Dubrowski slumped in the rocking chair I have in my office. Made I guess for especially stupendous gay students. It was really rocking when he told me he had considered not hiding his identity any longer. "With the entire family visiting at Thanksgiving, it would be a perfect time to tell them I am gay." "I have two words for you – Catholic and Polish. They will never understand. You will gain nothing and lose everything. Anyway, there is no perfect time and Thanksgiving is the worst possible time. Only announcing your gayness on your mother's death bed would be worse." I begged him to reconsider. He was determined. I was horrified at the pending catastrophe.

An ominous preview of the family catastrophe would have occurred if he had told his clique first. The four-member clique had been together since kindergarten. The clique was shattered. (A) was a socially conscious entrepreneur. If he ever met Johnny again, he would have walked right by him. Johnny didn't exist any longer. (B) was a devout Roman Catholic. Never cared to contact Johnny. Would have been nervous and uncomfortable around him. Avoided contact. (C) was an athlete and outdoorsman. Built rock walls. Supported and protected Johnny. Often visited him in Vancouver.

The turkey was soaking in cold water in the sink. The stick of dynamite was hidden inside the turkey. Johnny Dubrowski was about to light the dynamite when his sister announced she was six weeks pregnant. There was such joy, hugs and kisses. Jubilation. Johnny Dubrowski lit the turkey anyway.

Someone somewhere pushed the mute button. The family became a photograph. Except the father. He pulled the chair out from under Johnny. Picked him up off the floor like a bundle of laundry. Dragged him across the kitchen. Lifted him to his feet. Shoved him so fiercely against the refrigerator that all the magnets flew off the door and were strewn all across the kitchen.

"GET OUT. YOU ARE NO SON OF MINE. YOU PERVERT."

The father stomped upstairs to Johnny's room, opened the window, and threw his things out on the lawn.

Some of the neighbours helped Johnny pick up some of his stuff that could be salvaged. It was raining.

Johnny rode the night bus to Vancouver.

As far as I know, he never visited the little town again.

A bedroom full of trophies

The house lights dim. The conductor works his way through the orchestra to the podium. He taps the edge of the music stand. Raises the baton, poised, and as it crashes down, so begins the musical 'A Life Of Good Times'.

The red velvet curtain slowly opens to a magnificent scene. The stage is dominated by a gigantic ski hill. But the ski hill is not a slope but white stairs. The white stairs lead to the pinnacle where there is a silver arch and, on the crescent, these golden letters 'The House of the Gods.' Hanging from the arch is a huge silver star and in the center of the star is a picture of our hero: Jonathon

Aloysius Foley. 'JAY' FOLEY! The glaring white spotlight shines continually on the star. It never dims.

The trumpets blare as Jay steps in front of his star. He is dressed in a regal ski outfit. Scarlet. The male dancers rush onto the stage. They are dressed in a carnival array of glowing colors. The ski hill is painted with them. No one else wears scarlet.

Onto the stage rolls seven teachers' desks. Atop each desk a teacher is blindfolded and tethered. The dancers are wild with excitement and joy.

When the spotlight moves down the ski hill steps, the desks slide off stage. Jay's dance is furious but futile. The spotlight will not let him dance up the steps. In fact, the spotlight moves him down the ski hill until Jay is dancing on the stage itself.

Jay's star falls from the arch and slides down the ski hill as the spotlight blacks out. Just then half the ski hill slides to stage right. From the back of the stage, out of its shadows, rolls a giant golden trophy. It opens. Out of the trophy dances scantily glad women and naked men in black speed-dos. An orgy ensues.

One by one the male dancers return, now dressed in black ski outfits. One by one they take their positions on the ski hill. They do not move. The orgy slows and it too stops.

On a bottom step of the ski hill, a scarlet cloak has been spread. Jay, still dressed in his scarlet ski outfit, lays sprawled. He dies. From the rafters a giant sign glide down. It glows with hundreds of yellow light bulbs, spelling, GOOD TIMES. The light bulbs begin to flash as the red velvet curtain slowly closes.

I am holding a sports article I clipped from The Mountain View News that appeared the week after Jonathon Aloysius Foley killed himself in the snow at Summit Lake. In bold letters, the headline read "A LIFE OF GOOD TIMES". There beneath the headline was the file photo of the smiling handsome Jay Foley holding one of his many trophies. The reporter gushed about all his victories, friends, travels, parties. Is the reporter just stupid or am speaking a different language? If Jay's life was full of such good times, why did he put a bullet through his heart? Near the end, the reporter mentioned Jonathon Aloysius Foley died of a bullet wound. Where were these headlines?

JAY FOLEY CUT FROM CANADIAN NATIONAL SKI A TEAM
FOLEY REJECTED FROM CANADIAN NATIONAL B TEAM

JAY FOLEY LOSES SKI SCHOLARSHIP AT THE UNIVERSITY OF NEW MEXICO

JAY FOLEY FAILS COLLEGE ENTRANCE EXAMS

LONG TIME GIRLFRIEND DUMPS SKI CHAMPION

No, our reporter is not stupid. All he did was believe the myth of the Golden Boy Ski Champion. Many did. There is plenty of blood on plenty of hands. The town needs a gallon of Lady Macbeth's detergent. A high school administration who was willing to graduate a functioning illiterate. High school teachers willing to excuse absents, ignore assignments, write special exams. Adoring classmates charmed by his nonchalance. A father mesmerized by his son's persona. A mother fearful, but ultimately overwhelmed. And blood on my hands. I was willing to file his disastrous test results so as not to break his spirit. We had a term to teach him to read and write.

Once a hero, now, the foil becomes a nincompoop. The town wasn't so much disappointed as embarrassed. The father railed against the eastern establishment. Folks listened politely and then remembered all the booze Jay consumed and the drugs Jay injected. Jay thought he would still be renowned a loser – come on! But Jay never really did get use to those nervous awkward stares. At times he would turn thinking he heard the High school Marching band and those gals shaking those scarlet pompoms. His color.

Oh, man, when he was KING! When Jay skied down the slopes, other skiers would stop and gape and gasp. His speed. His grace. His intuition. He was like a bolt of lightning skiing down the runs. Surely, he is destined to be an international skiing sensation. But… To many smiles, not enough sweat. The possibilities shrank (with his physique and gaze, après ski attire contract for sure) as his partying became more notorious. (for sure a Coors Beer commercial in a Swiss chalet). I'm joking – of course. Still…

A few years after Jay's death, the Foleys divorced. It was obvious, he loved his son more than he loved his wife. In their grief, they couldn't find each other again. She moved to the island; he didn't move at all. He disappeared even if there wasn't a crowed to disappear into. It wasn't skiing. He would have supported his son in whatever he wanted to do. They loved each other.

"They loved each other." That's what a music student told me. He is a drummer from Saskatchewan. Mr. Foley advertised a basement suite. It was a good deal until Mr. Foley showed him Jay's bedroom. The room was not disturbed since his son's death. He was still alive in all the trophies, medals, photographs. It was just too creepy.

An old sagging couch slip covered in bright shiny marigolds on a pearl blue background

It is… Only four thirty, but the winter darkness had the black of midnight. Will there ever be a spring? Although this dark dreary afternoon could not have been a better atmosphere for discussing 'Doctor Faustus''. I wondered… when God pitched Mr. Lucifer and his bawdy crew out of heaven and down into Hell's depths, did they fall with their music – Their cosmic symphony. Definitely. It became jazz. There isn't a jazz musician in all of heaven which includes the cloud nine lounge. Harp music ever since.

As I turned to enter my office, I saw Logan Doyle sitting in the rocker. Not rocking. Tense. Did he get one of the girls in Marcella Hall, the girl's dorm, pregnant? Probably. He is over there enough. They should call the dorm Doyle's Haul. Out front is a bronze statue of the world war one nurse, Marcella. Rather large boobs for early twentieth century, I always thought. I didn't say anything. Decorum you know.

"I need to talk to you before tomorrow."

The part of Logan Doyle is played by Logan Doyle. There is no acting in this last piece in our long wordy sojourn. I will tell you exactly what he told me. I owe him that much.

Logan was dressed as Logan anyway. New running shoes. He had recently won 20,000.00 smackers in a 6/49 scratch and win. Still the same old torn Levi's. And wears a Harley Davidson t-shirt. Always a size too small. To show off the ripple of his muscles. He had a thick heavy mop of shiny black hair that he never combed. It drove the ladies crazy.

Logan told me once that when he made love, he entered into a trance becoming once again a little boy exploring the mystery of a woman's body. The pumping of his penis became the drum beat of childbirth. In his hands, in his touch, in the nakedness of his body, the child glowed in the womb. Its innocence protected from time and its world.

"Tomorrow, at eight thirty, the RCMP will arrest me."

I wanted to say "Arrest?" But I could say nothing.

"So today is the last day of my old life. I will lose everything I call myself and will lose everyone in my life. Even you will treat me differently tomorrow. Tomorrow, I have a new fate, a fate where I am shunned by everyone."

What in the hell did you do? I wanted to ask. But I could say nothing.

"I have pleaded guilty to one account of child molestation."

Many, many human beings have sat in that rocker over the years and some have spoken of the evil they encountered. There was the woman whose father was a wealthy famous international model. But inside his beauty was a violent beast. Once, when she was a little girl, to taunt his estranged wife, he put one hand over her mouth so she couldn't scream, and with the other hand, shoved a pencil into her thigh.

There was the woman who showed me that day's Vancouver sun. The oldest son had taken a gun and killed everyone in the house. He was arrested. For a while the families lived next door to each other. I was visiting his mother when I went into the kitchen for a glass of water. He was five and sitting alone playing with a large metal hook and ladder truck. When he saw me, he shoved the fire truck forcefully forward. It slammed into my foot cutting the skin. It bled a bit. He said nothing. But he grinned, except there was no grin on his face. It was his stare that frightened me. It sliced right through the shivers in me. I was staring at the devil. I left. Said nothing. Never went into that house again. I should have said something. But would they have believed me.

But this was different.

Evil was sitting in my office. A child had been harmed. He was lascivious. I felt a chill tremble my body. Who was in my office? Logan Doyle who I have known. Or? A demon. Who possessed the body of Logan Doyle? How could he? Did he actually take pride in his possession? How did he get this way? Could he ever be saved? I was afraid to look at him. Afraid of his eyes on me. With his strength, he could at any moment leap forward and strangle me. Calm down.

Calm down, I did. Logan Doyle was helpless. He had won the fight but lost the battle. An invisible tumour of evil lived inside his brain. And that evil could at any time, when it wanted too, possess him.

The moment of his truth had arrived. 'Le Momento de Verdad' to the Spanish, their soul is the essence of the bull ring, and the essence of the bull ring is when the matador, with just his sword, faces, alone, the horns of a crazed bull. The bull is wounded, humiliated, knowing he will die soon. The bull is now most dangerous. His charges are staggering, unpredictable.

With his will, the matador must control the nature of the beast, and the beast inside himself. As the sword slips quickly over the horns of the already dead bull, man has beaten the baseness of his animal nature. It is man's supreme moment. If, that is, man can understand the moment's meaning for his own life in that spiritual bull ring. 'The Corrido de Toros' – The Spanish are a very passionate people. They are in love with the very darkness in the soul of their mad passions.

Logan Doyle enters the bull ring. There waits his father – Carl Doyle. The part of Carl Doyle is played by Carl Doyle. He wanted the part. He is the purest form of evil. He doesn't want to escape his self even if he was given the chance. He loves what he does, who he is. It is his great frightening strength. Salvation be damned.

"My father first sexually assaulted me when I was, I guess four. It was in the basement, always the basement. Basements are my doom. As I got older, my father became my sexual mentor. I thought that is what sons do. The beatings, the fuckings, became more sadistic, more brutal. I began to train. I would become so strong that I could destroy him as he had ruined me. I guess I was seventeen. I heard him down in the cellar. I grabbed him and beat the shit out of him. I just used my fists. I was resurrected. I ripped all his clothes off. Threw him over the workbench and fucked him till I had nothing left. I left him in his squalor."

Carl Logan fled so fast that he left behind his Harley. I should have gotten rid of that machine. It was him and him had me whenever I rode it. I didn't know that. Mom never knew what he had done to me. She wouldn't have understood. What could she have done? Nothing. In about six months, she ran off with a chip truck driver. Never have seen or heard from her since.

"I had already moved out. I had the attic room and some board at this pub. My job was to clean the pub after the last drunk left. But I also had my own business. I gave massages to ladies and some gentlemen in my room. Washing the sheets of semen, the only chore."

Logan had enough money saved to try college. He was eighteen. He realized beating his father was not the confrontation that would free him. It had to be a face-to-face confrontation. The father was in prison for armed robbery. So, on his way to the little college town, Logan stopped at the prison. Logan Doyle's moment of truth had arrived.

All that Logan can remember is his father laughing. Ridiculing him. He was no longer eighteen. He was eight. He forgot what he wanted to say. Carl Logan said it all.

"Your mother may have given birth to you, but I created you. I taught you how to suffer pain. How to unfold your body in a fuck. I am you. You are me. And in time, you will be on this side of the glass."

Logan wanted out. He dropped the phone. Fled the prison. Climbed on his father's Harley. The roar of the engine caused a surge of sexual glee. He rode the Harley until it ran out of fuel. Then he left the Harley on the side of the road and walked away

"I should have seen the basement suite as a trap, but the rent was cheap, and I needed a place. She is a single mom with two daughters – seven and ten. She despises her ex, but probably lost the custody battle because of her intense hatred. Her ex gets the girls one week end a month. She is suspicious – worried. Pride vilified, her ex holds grudges and connives. On those tense once a month weekends, the ten-year-old is forced to sleep on the divan. The seven-year-old sleeps in a queen size bed with the father. The door is always locked."

"If the basement wasn't a trap, the orange couch was definitely nightmarish. It was cheap. Free. Nobody bought it at the Estate Sale. They even delivered the orange couch tied to the roof of this Volkswagen van. She finally bought a slip-cover for the sagging behemoth. The flowers looked carnivorous, the background tawdry."

"I was lounging on the tired old behemoth wearing my Harley tee shirt and a pair of shorts. The young one climbs in my lap with her dragon book and I cuddle her in my arm. As I read, she teases me seductively. Her little fingers creep under my Harley and quickly find my navel and soon are enmeshed in my pubic hair. I am amazed at her promiscuity. The urge becomes insurmountable."

NO! Don't. I don't want to know.

"She tells her third-grade teacher about the man in the basement who has a funny way of touching her."

As Logan leaves my office, he joins a group of his friends heading to the gym for a badminton tournament. He is lingering on the edge of never. Tomorrow, the college will be shocked. I have a dark drive home. Thinking of Doctor Faustus. Thankful to be going home.

In the next few years, letters arrive from Logan. In the transfer prison, he lost weight. The inmates hate child molesters. Glass shards in his scrambled eggs. Apple juice tainted with piss. At the Wilkshire prison for social deviates, he spent eight months as a janitor. Alone. Talked to no one. Evasive in group sessions and diabolically sincere with the institute psychiatrist. Eight months of moping and remorse, Logan Doyle was on his newly purchased Harley. The job was mundane, but the girl was in love and dreamed of marrying him. She would be reviled if she knew his past. He was certain about that. He got on his Harley and roared off. Where it would happen all over again? THE LETTERS STOPPED. A teacher is haunted by the ghosts who live inside his memories.

Gone never to return, so religion offers this farewell as a eulogy to Logan Doyle. Requiem aeternam dona eis, domine; et lux perpetua luceat eis. (Eternal rest grant to them, O Lord, and let perpetual light shine upon them.) Hah. Hah.

Twenty-Seven

The last chapter of a human life is the most difficult to write. Only language remains and new voices speak new meanings to old words. Left a drift… to the silence on coming. Besides the withering of the body, the brain – in dead and dying neuron cells – shrinks the skein and sense of the self. Growing old is like becoming a clown – of course without the face paint and clodhopper red shoes. The way you walk (shuffle). The way you talk (hoarse). The way you think (nostalgic). So, the image in the mirror is unrecognizable. Where did "I" go? Where will "I" go? The end of life like its beginning needs to be swaddled in care and comfort… The touch of a hand will last an eternity.

Twenty-Eight

Approximately Three O'Clock

It whizzed by twiddling my ear. Hit the back blackboard, splattering. A Condom. Super-size. Then again the size of the banana was impressive. The siege of the ATLAS Super-size condoms had its first volley. May no class ever again endure such raw terror. Even to this very day, whenever I am in that classroom, I glance to see if the stain is still there on the back blackboard. It is! And I am glad to be alive with just a twiddling.

George stood defiant yet nervous behind four boxes of super-size condoms (Goliath. Samson. Godzilla. And Wallop – a cheap brand from Bangcock, sold at Gateway Grocers. They were hidden between Kleenex tissues and Bounty paper towels). And beside the boxes, lies a plump ripe yellow banana that would have made any Italian gigolo proud. George grabbed the muscular banana with gusto, flexing his obvious chauvinistic masculinity. The demonstration speeches for the Business Administration students had commenced. George chose an interesting topic but not very relevant. The majority of students had learned how to use a condom in Mister Roger's Neighborhood. The very yellow banana was slippery and George's hands sweaty, and even trembling (I might add). His first rocket had whistled between me and a screaming damsel now a distressed Marketing Major.

A student yells. "George has loaded another cannon."

FIRE! FIRE!

Some students had ducked under the classroom tables; others raised their text books as shields. The only time some of the students had ever bothered to open their text books. Smack! Smack! Yelp! Yelp!

George had become crazed with determination. He would not be defeated by a Gateway Grocer's On Sale Banana. The ceiling fluorescent light fixtures were now a hanging garden of spent condoms. When I called Maintenance to bring a ladder to M20, they didn't even question why. Speech Class. Exclamation point Question Mark (! ?)

We once used the Nursing Department classroom. But the nursing department never really forgot the shattering. Their grinning skeleton, Jeffery, who stood guard at the rear of the classroom and frightened first year speakers, was shattered by a Wallop bull's-eye. His bones shattered everywhere. Jeffery's grin was never quite the same.

But what alarmed the class was the condom George in desperation chose next. A Wallop with a musical chip embedded in the tip, so when push came to shove, the condom played music. George had chosen – and quite rightfully – (wouldn't you stand at attention and even salute) – the Military Services Marching Band's patriotic rendition of "Oh Canada".

It wouldn't stop playing, perched dangling on the light fixture. You couldn't knock it down. It got louder and louder. Drums and bugles marching ever forth until a text book killed it. A direct hit. The condom fizzled! Plopping then flopping like a dying fish. OOOOOHHHHH C A N A D A!

Unfortunately, the class ended in a blood bath. George chose a "Godzilla" Monster Condom. Thank God Gateway Grocers don't sell "ZEUS" condoms. Godzilla shot upward directly into his face. There was a sexual gasp from many in the class, including to my surprise the petite marketing major. George was led from the classroom with a fat wad of toilet paper pressed against his right bleeding eyebrow. George had five stitches sewed in his right eyebrow. George was required to reconstruct the ever smiling Jeffery. He did. But they never found Jeffery's penis. For what it is worth, I have never trusted Marketing majors.

I still remember seeing on the desk – forlorn – the yellow banana. Its nub was cracked and a white cream was oozing out.

Twenty-Nine

Two O'Clock on a Sweltering Desert Morning

LARA!

Laralaralara!

She had written (*I am still going through Mom's stuff. You gave her a rock and the attached letter. What's that all about.*) Then, I wrote back (*It is not "just" a rock. It is a special rock. The rock is from Elephant Mountain. And it has special healing powers. Mystical powers! It can heal your soul of its sorrow. Sorrow wounds. It cuts deeply into our ability to believe in some telltale myth that explains – to us – our existence.*)

NO!

Not really.

"Elephant Mountain Mystical Rocks" was all a prank. From so long ago. I had almost forgotten. In hindsight, I grant you the prank was quite quaint and laughable in its gullibility. So I gather you got the joke. Whose fault is it that you're not a believer? And why am I defending myself against a heretic? But your suspicious questioning reveals your awareness of the outlandish claptrap used to tempt human nature to believe! Now in my forties and ensconce in my decadent hubris, I feel quite comfortably secure in my sincere cynicisms. Devote Sarcasm…

At night, in bed, all alone, I can confront the nothingness that is death with much courageous bravado. Die? I am not afraid of dying. Then, I realize I will never see these people standing around my death bed again. Never watch their lives evolve. Never know who the murderer is of the half-read mystery story. These people were the cast of characters in the play that was my life. Now that I will soon be gone from time, they will remember me only as the bits and pieces of who I am/was. And the last thing you want to do is exit stage, right? No life is ever complete. There is always something else. And you won't be there to…. The prank isn't quite so funny any longer. Lara, I think you could use right now an eternal story with its appropriate happy ending. I'm not proud. Anything will do. Even a little incense. A sprinkling of holy water. Sure, why not some chanting?

Lara, the gods have been excruciatingly cruel to you. To lose a mother and a young son in the same month of December leaves this clown gagged, with a gargle of words in his mouth. And then I remembered this woman from Dusseldorf. I was in Cuba. It was early, on a very gray morning. The sun hadn't risen yet. The day had not begun officially, nor had night technically left. I was walking along the beach. Actually… I was looking for a private place to piss… when this woman comes up beside me. This was her last morning in Cuba. Her Lufthansa flight to Frankfurt left at eleven. When not walking along a beach, she was a lawyer (Mergers and Acquisitions). She loved beaches. They were a true democracy. Life reduced to a bathing suit. All your money, all your talent, all your sins become a mere set of footprints immediately washed away.

The woman from Dusseldorf was intrigued that I had just retired from a career of teaching English. Then, she did it. She wasn't being mean – at least I don't think she was. The woman asked "that" unforgiveable question. "After all of the books you have read, did any one of them teach you the meaning of life?" I had no idea what to say. Blank! Well, it wasn't even six o'clock! I am quick as a whip at seven! I wanted to drown myself. But that would ruin a placid sea and for once a cloudless sky. And I still had to piss. I felt worthless. But I knew I had to come up with something. I was desperate. I thought of Camus even Melville. The grey existential morning was just too obvious. She being a lawyer and all. After hemming and hawing and qualifying like crazy, I heard myself say "Pirandello's The Man With A Flower In His Mouth". Thank god the woman from Dusseldorf didn't know Pirandello and so I could blather onward wondering how much of my career was pure blather.

For you Lara, and because of those gods you have somehow angered, I will answer that evil question truthfully. (Probably, you won't believe me.) (Once a prankster always a prankster.) (Anyway, there are plenty of choices around.) (So take your pick.) (My pick is next.)

A BEAUTIFUL WORK OF ART

In sculpture. In paint. In dance. In music. In words. In images. In architecture. And yet in one of these arts that attracts you, you will hear, like the roar of the sea in a conch shell, the universe calling out the answer to that question so surreptitiously hidden so long long ago, inside the universe itself. Wrapped in the sheen of the Milky Way Galaxy.

But if I did have to choose a particular work of art, I would choose for my work of art a large boulder among a crowd of rocks on our beach. It was shaped like a giant fish. And it was smiling. Depending on the lake level, it swam blissfully. Other times it drown beneath the waves. Somehow there occurred a six inch crack on one side that had collected dirt and dust and needles. Over time a tiny tree spouted, but with so little sustenance and too much water it shriveled. No matter. I had my very own Fisher King from the Arthurian Legend and found my own search for the Holy Grail. The Fisher King is a symbol of prosperity and healing. I knew then, way way back then, a fanciful then, that no matter what would happen in the lives of our family, it would be all right. Eventually. And it has been. All Right. Eventually.......

And, Lara, it will be all right for you, too. Once you rid yourself of their belongings and have the courage to say goodbye, forgetting their things and remembering their selves. To be blunt, I feel the tone of your email, Lara, is blatantly accusatory. Of what I am not quite sure. So, comic mockery does not sit well in a coffin. That makes me culpable? Maybe you should reread my profound encyclical. If blame is to be meted out, then, you can blame our house – a party house. The house is cursed you know. I learned that from Albert of "Charles Hair Salon" – after I bought the house of course. The last two owners divorced after their husbands ran off with a toasty blonde (Albert's words). Still....... I am waiting for the next available toasty blonde to come sauntering by.

There are some things in life you are not allowed to have. I guess for me it is a toasty blonde. But I do own a large pink boat house that came with the property. I didn't even check it out. I couldn't afford a raft much less a boat. Supposedly, the last owner swam naked across the lake at seven every morning. So Albert said and Albert knows everything that happens in town. A barber's chair is as revealing of life's little truths as a confessional box. You cannot resist talking, talking, talking. Although Albert failed to mention what was in the boat house.

Yes, he did mention the chubby papa Otter who often slept in the boat house to get away from his noisy family. He certainly didn't mention "that" other stuff.

Two Saturdays later a Boy Scout appears at our door. "Any bottles?"

"No, not here, but you may find a few bottles in the boat house. No! I didn't paint it pink! It was red at one time. And watch out for the Otter. Bang the door twice."

The boy scouts filled two pickup trucks full of beer bottles that had over the years been neatly stacked from floor to ceiling. It explained to me how the past owner could swim naked across the lake at seven in the morning – every morning too… Then again the Otter may have been a drunk.

Not only the typical Pacific Northwest log cabins but also your wooden "A" Frame cottages seldom permitted a Mediterranean Villa in their midst. Like our domicile. Built by old man Gruthers in the thirties – nineteen thirties. Gruthers was the head engineer who planned those new fangled asphalt highways that brought us interlopers into his tranquility. Picayune like crazy, in Autumn especially, old man Gruthers would not allow a single leaf to lie on his lawn. Unattended. He and his faithful rake quickly grabbed each culprit. His yard, his house, his life were pristine. His creepy bi-speckled wife would hide in the shrubs to watch me weed, as if I would steal any of their weeds. Unnerving those beady tiny eyes. Also unnerving, Mr. and Mrs. died on the same day – just hours apart. They never spent a cent they didn't have too, so they are probably quite snug in the same pine coffin and a single silk lavender pillow so the etched wrinkles of these two pioneers were soften. Without a family (they outlived everyone), the estate was willed to the Legion Hall where he often caroused with the boys from the regiment. The leaves that November of their passing had a field day, pooping all over his yard. His trusty rake rusting. Lara, as you well know, we always leave something behind. Digging around the beach one afternoon, I found the metal tub from the original Gruthers house. What are you keeping? (Besides, of course, the gray rock)

Out of all the stuff you intend to pitch out. I bet you haven't decided or haven't understood the significance of your decision. Of the many many things dad left behind, I only kept a rotted wooden walkway of old green shingles. It helps me to remember him. I don't know why? I knew very little about his life. He was a quiet solitary man. For sure, "That" keeping will help you let go of your grief for your mom. And YES your guilt. That's really none of my business.

But I think I know where, especially the guilt comes from. And of course I will tell you later. Eventually.

Well, you are the one who asked. Your mom told me something that you don't know. Yes, I asked her why she didn't tell you and I know definitely she would never tell your brother. All families have secrets which of course are never mentioned at the funeral. The ideal of the corpse always outlives his or her years. Even his or her rancid farts fade in time.......

Furthermore, on the scale of uniqueness, our house rings ten bells, since it climbs the rump of Elephant Mountain. Each room is on a higher level. Escher would have loved it. It required yeoman effort to climb the 57 steps starting at the garage to reach the double bed in the tower loft. I am surprised we ever conceived children. It was definitely a party house. We seldom disappointed our guests. Especially at Easter. The party was to decorate this giant ornamental cherry tree with some 125 blow up bunnies and over 700 balloons. Mostly found rampaging through flea markets. (500 hundred giant balloons for five dollars. Printed on each "Doris Loves Ted". No, I have no shame.) It all started and I won't say why with 4 bunnies and 8 balloons. Oh, why not. The decorations were to remember my cousin's wife who decorated balloons painted to look like fancy Russian Easter Eggs and died from a virulent breast cancer a week before Holy Saturday. It was a memorial to a delight who decorated our mundane lives once a year

Our house became known as the Bunny House. When we left that October for Australia, the cherry tree was yellow with dying leaves. When we walked out of the Baggage Claim at the Auckland Airport, their ornamental cherry tree was pink with blossoms. The planet is definitely weird.

Lara's mom could not have received the grey rock at our Chocolate Party held one Christmas long ago. Lara's mother "Sandy" (Sandra) was living in Phoenix. We had over 75 guests and more than a hundred types of chocolate displayed all over the house. Yes, including the bathroom. Our dog snatched most of the brownies from the coffee table. The sweetest poop the world has ever known.

Since cacao was considered the food of the gods and ironically a bitter aphrodisiac, nonetheless, chocolate was central to the religious rituals of the Olmec, Aztec, Inca civilizations. Jesus sweetened the old testament despot just as Hershey sugared the modern religious taste. The Kootenays are noted for their springs of spirituality popping up on almost all burbling creeks. If chocolate is holy, then I should have no problem creating my own cult out of Elephant Mountain rocks. Oh but the Gods had a surprise for this amateur prophet. Nordstrom donated eighty small elegant silver and royal blue boxes. Inside wrapped in tissue paper was a gray Elephant Mountain rock. Folded in the bottom of the box was a single sheet explaining the ritual. (And the guests assumed they were receiving as they left the party a rich chocolate treat of splendid sexual pleasures.) And I owned a whole mountain of grey rocks, well, almost whole, to pawn off as miraculous icons.

The single sheet read: ....(This section is not for you, Lara, but for the others who might someday be reading this mix of memories.) *You are in the process of transferring your grief and burdens of regrets to this sleeping giant that the First People trusted and respected. And thus you can be free of your troubles. For a while, anyway. Elephant Mountain allows you not to attain redemption. Just relief! Choose a comfortable chair to sit in quietly... Don't worry about house noises. Place the rock in the palm of your hand. If you are young imagine yourself elderly. If you are old, remember those days of youthful exuberance and indolence. Time should vanish now so you can become a child suspended in the darkness of infinite space. Now, gently fold your fingers around the small rock. You will feel a warmth emanating from the stone. Now place your other hand on top. Soon, inside your mind a kaleidoscope of images and scenes will appear. Relax! Elephant Mountain has absorbed all your woes. The last vista is your rock joined with the First People in the great circle of their ancient rocks. Every year they would bring their rock, their life, and place their being in the great circle. Then, they would account for the happenings that year. It was like a clock without hands. Sorrow belongs to all people. The Elephant has learned this over many many centuries and will always guard your sadness and its secrets.*

But Lara your Mom was not supposed to receive a grey rock. Much much too humdrum for a budding religion. All religions worth their scroll story require opulent pageantry and jeweled paraphernalia. So we can't see the truth that all religions hide from their penitent. It's Holy Fakery sent directly from the gods. Heavenly Beamed. The only reality is the reflection of the faces of the poor in the sheen of the golden collection plate.

Holly Molly! What an amateur I am! A gray rock? Never! It would be like hanging the corpse of a convict from the sanctuary crucifix instead of the svelte muscular body of the handsome Jesus Christ – draped seductively in a loin cloth.

Elephant Mountain is a heap of gray rock. So very old. It is almost beyond time. You drop one rock atop another gray rock and it shatters like the bones of a frail old man. I needed a glamorous rock with pizzazz. I needed a drive to Eliot's Roost where the last of two lighthouses beacon. They are the relics of a bygone era of the stern wheelers. Replaced with asphalt highways and trestles with iron rails. These ships of such stately beauty, that had lugged tons of silver and gold, were ignominiously paddled to the middle of Kootenay Lake where they were set afire and drown in their own light. A few remain beached and rotting. History ticks a wicked clock.

When their light bulbs burnt out, their bulbs were not replaced. The light houses were sold at auction. Now they are cherished, yes, History is that fickle. The light house at Phineas Rockery would welcome vessels from Kootenay lake into Kootenay Bay; the lighthouse at Eliot's Roost would wave a fair well. The only ships to sail the bay these days are a car ferry and pleasure craft who are still tormented by the unruly winds that zigzag down the valleys.

Eliot's lighthouse sits on Pebble Creek Beach. Full of colored pebbles. Hues of reds, yellows, and browns. Shards constantly washed down from the copper and iron streaked in Whiskey Mountain. Just what a nascent religious cult needs. Neon Magic. But there is an irony here. I had long ago emptied my jar of Whiskey Mountain pebbles. Something quite grim must have happened for me to send your Mom a gray rock. It was grim. Lara you can ignore the next section.

I knew you wouldn't.

I knew your Mom and Dad before you were born. When they were young. Just starting their careers. Just finding the path toward each other. It was July. This is important. It happened on a July night where the sun light lingers as the shadow of the opposite mountains climb slowly into night. I was shocked at how little I knew about my parents. I was shocked at how little I wanted to know. I don't know about you. What were we like that July night? When we were young, twenty five or so, and free, and just tasting the excitement of the adventure ahead. Not afraid when we should have been very afraid. They are us and we are them. Maybe that is why we don't want to know. Particulars.

On that July night it happened while playing a game of Monopoly that was no longer a game for your parents but a denunciation of their marriage. For my wife and I an embarrassment and trepidation. Before the game begins, let me tell you where and who each of the players are. The silver metal Monopoly tokens that were selected to pass GO and collect $200.00!

The Racing Car Token. Bradley James (Sky King) DiBello. Husband. Married to Sandra. A swaggering HE. A He who barges into a room and with his charisma assumes control. He has the physique of a football player and the magnetism of a mafia God Father. Generous and congenial. He dominates women with his hungry sensuality. In the waning light at the edge of the beach and lake, Bradley, shirtless, sands an old wooden row boat. His muscles in rhythm with the curvature of the boat. No one could tell, not even Bradley, the depth of his passion for flying. It would determine his fate. It was all there in his Valedictory Address, but nobody – especially Sandra – was actually listening. In a few days the DiBellos would venture North. Sky King had accepted a desk job as principal of a grade school.

Top Hat. Guest. English Teacher. Standing in the living room staring out at the lawn that slopes to the beach watching one of his most successful students who will charm his way through all those people problems.

The Wheelbarrow. Wife. Sandra McPhee. Emergency Room Nurse. Stands beside the Top Hat talking. Bradley forgot to thank Sandra in his Valedictorian Address. It was in the written text. He just missed it. She paid for his education and he carelessly spent their fortune. The pseudo god father always had to pick up the check. At first, I thought The Wheelbarrow was a patsy overwhelmed by the jungle hero of a cartoon adventures. But the Wheelbarrow was smart and determined. Sagacious. She was dominated by authoritarian men beginning with her father. Her mother died when she was quite young. She was attracted to their power.

The Thimble. Guest. Teacher. Wife of the Top Hat… In the kitchen preparing a tray of fancy hor'durves. Lara, the Thimble understood more than you the burden you carried. Our journeys over the decades would occasionally cross. The thimble was amused how the daughter had the physique of the father but the temperament of the mother whereas the son Ricky had the body of the mother but a despotic need to rule – like the ever demanding never satisfied father. Nothing lower than an "A+" was acceptable.

A JULY NIGHT MONOPOLY GAME

The Racing Car sped around the board throwing doubles and buying everything in sight, The Racing Car had plenty of properties, but a slim stack of bucks. Houses, and especially Hotels, are expensive! The Thimble kept landing on railroads and utilities. Not much profit and she kept her unlucky streak with utility taxes. The Thimble was actually relieved to be bankrupt. The Thimble had a degree in mathematics, but had read plenty of literature to know just how fictitious numbers can be. The Thimble noticed a tension between Bradley and Sandy, Constant snipe ping. Gleeful denunciations when the die turned ugly. The Thimble kicked the Top Hat under the card table. The Top Hat had already been mulling over some excuses to leave. The Top Hat's luck was swank – and sinister. The Top Hat bought both Boardwalk and Park Place and a few hotels and waited to fleece his customers. The players avoided the Ritz as if word had spread that the properties were infested with bed bugs . His fortune dwindled. Then, it happened. The mulled over excuses weren't necessary…

The Racing Car flung the die across the Monopoly Board. The tumbling die smashed into a stack of Community Chest Cards. One die had six dots. The other die, also had six dots showing, but it had slid off the board, now lying diagonally across the card table and the .Monopoly Board. The Racing Car had escaped the Wheelbarrow's richest properties. But……. The throw was illegal. Rules state the die must come to rest on the board. The Bitch enjoyed – sorry, the Wheelbarrow, enjoyed pointing this inconvenient rule – the applicable rule. The rules were wadded and tossed under the card table. We thought of running for the door. His next throw –not so lucky. One die read three, the other die, four. It meant a very expensive stay at a hotel infested piece of property. The Racing Car had mortgaged most of his properties long vacant of any green houses and red hotels. His cash had dwindled so he could barely pay for a tank of gas. As he pathetically counted each of his dollars, The Racing Car would fight to the very last bitter penny. The greedy bitch /// sorry, Wheelbarrow. If Wheelbarrows could grin, this Wheelbarrow was definitely grinning. We glanced at the Mantel Clock. Oh my god look at the time. Eleven thirty, already. We grabbed for our jackets and salad bowl. Just then the Racing Car's large arm swept across the Monopoly Board scattering all the pieces across the porch.

Wipe Out!

We almost forgot the hor'durves tray. He was stomping around upstairs kicking his meagre belongings. Don't fret. He's Italian. Hates to lose. He always wins with his dick. Sex is our consolation prize. We helped Sandy pick up the pieces of their game. Realized the Get Out Of Jail Free Card was missing. Sandy searched everywhere, but never did find the "Get out of Jail Free" card. Did it get caught in our stuff? Nope! On our way home, the Top Hat and the Thimble wondered how those two found their way to each other. Unnerved, the securing home Monopoly tokens wondered if their love was somehow played out on that game board. For certain, they didn't need to wonder how the DiBello's discovered their way into each other's 'life... If the DiBello marriage lasts, it will because of Sandy McPhee's cash flow. I noticed searching for that damn jail card that she always kept her wealth secret – hidden on her lap. Life to Bradley was a slug fest; life to Sandy was fist-a-cuffs.

That weekend the DiBellos began their trek north to Fort Saint John. They soon loved the north. A land full of adventures, just waiting for its hero. Bradley was a very successful grade school principal. But the more successful the more bored Sky King became, and the more bored, the more outlandish the escape of adventure. So he cashed out their funds and built a fishing lodge and bought a used sea plane. Mostly rich Americans filled the registry. You had arrived, Lara, then your brother Ricky arrived to join the combustion of passions that was the DiBello household. It must have rained every day that Soggy Foggy Summer. The only dry item was the registration cancellation book/with quite a few red x's.

Wipe Out!

The next we heard, the DiBellos had moved to Phoenix. With a couple of aviation buddies, Sky King bought a small air cargo company located at Sky Harbor International. It all depended on contracts. Some months ended with cheap beers, other months ended with beef dinners. As usual, as that Monopoly game once demonstrated, like the future told by that sinister pack of Tarot cards, it (whatever it is) was predicted long ago. Too bad the Get Out Of Jail Free Card was never found. It changes life profoundly. Of course, Sandy McPhee kept the family from poverty. Her commissions bought quite a lot of Bradley's adventures and chunks of fillet minion. Sandy became a very successful realtor. **Mesa City Realtors.** *Sandy McPhee and Associates.* If you are asking, yes, he always insisted on picking up the check, and, no, he never thanked her. Sandy would often wonder when meeting a young couple how they disguised the jail that is their marriage. After a night when the animal had created his allure and had filled her kaleidoscope with a flurry of transcendent colors, she would wonder where that "Get Out Of Jail Card" had hidden itself. And. wondered what she would do if she ever found that card. Sandy McPhee understood money. She also understood love and romance. That is why she was so miserable.

Answer to the question of what it is like being a wheelbarrow. Wait! I guess I did actually forget the question. Not really. Lara! For a moment I had forgotten the beautiful simplicity of a human being. Often, what we remember about a person is some characteristic that is incidental or inexplicable. Through that feature we have come to know them and probably love them. Silly isn't it == but true. I have come to understand one Sandra McPhee, because she never ate leftovers. What wasn't eaten at dinner was pitched in the garbage. Sandy McPhee was very proud of that full garbage can.

Some memories arrive, and when they do, they explode in a thousand refractions of light. Not yet, Lara, one phone call to go. Stay with me, now. You won't be disappointed. You will learn how to love somebody. But a somebody you should have known how to love in the first place. All those preposterous testosterone emperor edicts of Sky King. But you didn't bother to understand them– you didn't care. If you had you would have found something besides the constant badgerings and hurt, something even beyond yourself. But Lara, you preferred to hate the buffoon instead. The Husband! The Father! But not surprisingly you didn't learn how to love the wife as she drove the covered wagon west fighting off Indians and cattle rustlers. Why bother? The only thing children learn from their parents is how to love. Once the child learns that the child moves on. Bradley and Sandy found a way to love each other or thought they did. Assumed a love, so they didn't bother to look around the edges. Slept next to a life size blow up doll who was taught how to say "I Love You," so eventually the fiction became a jailed realty. It should have frightened you Lara. That you should have been fooled so easily. That you didn't see how unhappy your mother was.

Our Valentine for today has one word inside: ***INERTIA***

Let the phone ring. Let the Thimble continue to slice the young one's weenies. Let the Top Hat glance at the TV screen sitting on top of a china cabinet. With their two daughters, let them watch the CBS Evening News with Walter Cronkite. Let the screen split into three photographs of men in their fifties. For a split second, let the Top Hat's spoon be suspended in midair poised to stir his coffee. Let him recognize one of the three men. Let him think he recognized one of the three. When did he go bald? Sky King himself. Bradley DiBello. The silver metal racing car Monopoly token. Let the three faces disappear to scenes of flooding around Austin Texas. Let him ask his wife what Walter just said. Let the phone ring.

"Bradley is dead!"

"I thought I recognized him."

"When did he go bald?"

"It nearly killed him. He bought every hair restorer he could find. Appearing young is the last muscle the aging Caruso excuses."

"How are the kids taking it?"

"Poorly!"

"Comic book heroes are not supposed to be blown to smithereens across the deserts of Northern Libya."

"Now who are the children going to rebel against?"

"Their mother."

"Probably"

"I never realized how heavy children can be until they cling to you wanting answers to questions not even asked and wanting the address of a different life. And I am having difficulty wearing the widow's weaves. I am light headed most of the time… I wake up at night laughing. It is just too rich. The lawyers tell us the settlement with the US Government will be substantial. If I invest wisely, I will never have to work again. It is just too rich. Sky King finally passed GO and collected more than $200.00. I will bury his body in Baltic Avenue. But the card I want is 'The Get Out of Jail Free' card. I guess that is not possible is it?"

"NO, Unfortunately, it is not. Not for beggars, not for kings. Not for angels with good or bad wings. Not for things like dreams. When everything else falls away, and it is you and the mirror, we mortals must depend on CHANCE."

Fate, Lara, did leave you and your brother and your Mother a Chance Card. A Chance Card in the form of a Marvel Superhero Comic Book. "**SKY KING AND THE LIBYAN REBELS. "**

Frame One: A vintage B-29 revs its four propeller driven engines. Once this relic filled its carcass with bombs. Now the antique is full of locust eradication equipment destined for the Sudan, so states the lucrative contract signed with US

AID. All three partners are like kids flying the beast. Airport eyes follow this historic bird until it disappears into today's reality. It's Alive!

Frame Two: When the B 29 Super Fortress lands in Algeria, one of its overheated four engines is smoldering. A small oil leak, easily corrected, solved the mechanical problem. Their flight plan had been approved by IAA in Phoenix. Algerian air space has confirmed the route of the B 29 North over the Sahara Desert instead of South over the Mediterranean Sea. Gibraltar Air Space has confirmed the delay. The B29 and its three pilots will depart at dawn for the Sudan No one notices the slip of paper that notes the change in the B 29 Flight Plan. It is now routed South along the Mediterranean and not North across the Sahara. Gibraltar does not notice the change. Algerian Air Control does not notice the change. Not one of the three pilots questions the change to the flight plan. They do notice the perfect flying weather. Not a cloud in the sky. They are excited to get the old bird airborne. Their flight plan will fly them directly over territory controlled by an armed group of Libyan rebels.

Frame Three: Junk that was once a Boeing B 29 Super Fortress that had survived the air war in the Pacific and endless air shows. The Libyan missile hit the old bird on the left hand side sheering off the engine that slammed into the exploding cockpit. One pilot was sipping coffee. One pilot was plotting a route around a storm front in the Sudan. One pilot was recording the readings of the numerous dials. That is all they remember. And they too were pieces of the falling junk.

Frame Four: No matter how many people, no matter how many times, they were told the pilots were unconscious at the combustion of the explosion, the nightmare that became Sky King's eulogy saw Bradley plummeting through a black funnel, suspended, never hitting the earth. Waking up to the howling of the wind and a silent scream that never ends the torment.

Now Playing! ***"FREE FALL"*** Not every night. But many a night. And now ten years later, seldom, not often at all. On this Anniversary, Sandra had done something terrible Unthinkable! She had to tell someone. Sandra McPhee picks up the phone and dials a number she hasn't phone in a long time.

Well, Lara, at last we are here. The phone by the kitchen table is about to ring, waking up the English Teacher who had fallen asleep over a stack of essays. Only he and their one eyed gold fish listen. They swear the gold fish had two eyes when they bought him at Woolworths. They named him Moyshe after the one eyed Israeli Defence Minister – Maysha Dayan. Whenever someone new arrives at the table, Moyshe swims over and burbles. Moyshe will understand what he will shortly hear. I am not so sure about the English Teacher.

Rings… the kitchen phone. Both Moyshe and Top Hat jump.

Sandra's mother died of pancreatic cancer when Sandra was thirteen. An intense and dominate love developed between the daughter and father. The father was at the top of a long list of dominant males that owned her. When she was a first year nursing student she fell in love with this Indian Doctor from Calcutta. Their love was tranquil and fierce. She accepted his proposal and engagement ring. Her father did not. The father was furious and adamant. The proposal was ultimately rejected. The father chose Bradley DiBello. The perfect son-in-law.

Love? —— Fill in the blank with your definition. It required most of the evening, but finally she had the Doctor's home phone number. Sandra McPhee begins to dial the number. If only the past could be as easily dialed and as easily discovered. No! recovered, so easily recovered. No-no! Can be as easily corrected as a poorly written sentence. Just how impossible is it to live a different past. Push button dreams. Dreams shouldn't be our only illusion. Stand alone in the sanctuary and cross yourself with these words "WHAT IF I HAD……." The only man she ever really loved was that Doctor from Calcutta. But the Doctor is 'happily married. But he has three daughters. But he is head of Pediatrics at Boston General. She stands as a solitary figure surrounded by a whirl of buts. The Doctor did remember. Her? Their love? She wanted to believe their love was once real, maybe forever real. But then does it really matter whether their love is as unattainable as one of those smiling photographs in an old picture album caught in the folds of your mind. They were happy for each other, or they sounded between the strained pauses happy for each other, and how their lives turned out. He was polite. She was contrite. She didn't know what to say but aware of what not to say.

The phone call lasted as long as a public hanging.

Your mother wanted you and your brother to find love in your marriages. Her fanatic determination that her children avoid a loveless marriage caused great animosity and the ruination of your first marriages. Lara Lara LARA!!! That is what she told me, and yet, could not stop herself from driving her children away.

Since our lives will probably never cross, nor do we actually want them too, please adopt that gray Elephant Mountain rock if you haven't already pitched it.

While sorting through your mother's belongings, look for a Monopoly Game. Who knows. That Get Out Of Jail Free Card might be somewhere in there.

HERE LIES AND THE OTHER FIBS OF ONE SANDRA MCPHEE WHO SPENT A LIFE TIME WITH A MAN SHE DID NOT LOVE… SHE OWES THE GODS NOTHING

LARA, ONE HOUR AFTER YOU HAVE FINALLY BURIED YOUR MOM, (AND THAT CAN TAKE YEARS) YOU WILL MEET YOUR MOM AT AN INTERSECTION WHERE AN "EARTH" PATH CROSSES AN "ETERNITY" PATH. FOR ONE HOUR, ETERNITY HAS CLOCKS TOO YOU KNOW, YOU AND YOUR MOTHER CAN TELL EACH OTHER WHAT YOUR LIVES WERE LIKE:. WAS LIKE, IS LIKE. THEN, YOUR MOTHER WILL DISAPPEAR INTO THE BEATIFICATION OF ETERNITY AND YOU WILL REAPEAR INTO THE THRUST OF YOUR OWN LIFE.

You're welcome

Thirty

Christmas Eve:

"There is No Womb in the Inn"

{It could happen} 26 hours is not enough time to separate two lives: A Washington D.C. college student (being) and a Wichita Kansas ranch house son (being). Actually it was only 13 hours ever since the deaf school rented an entire sleeper for themselves (and me). Blissful quiet from Washington to Chicago. Just the clickity clack rhythms of the Santa Fe's El Capitan and some soothing guitar strumming.

The Santa Fe arrived every Christmas in Wichita Kansas at exactly 5:29. No it didn't. It never arrived on time. Doesn't matter. Time stops at the prairies and doesn't begin again until you reach California.

There on the platform was the family waiting, gift wrapped in wool. Dad. Mom. Little brother. Our sister wasn't there because she was a nun (her choice). Good olde Methodist Dad became a Catholic for Mom's sake and not to have his only daughter imprisoned in a black and white Medieval costume. While on the other hand, it is advantageous having someone pleading with the Big Fellow to alleviate the guilt of owning a Motel which has guilt written all over it.

"Boy! You were surely born the son of an Inn Keeper." Bellowed by the craven Lawrence Lanigan. (Quite often snidely swiped as a matter of fact) I guess if you tallied all those Inn grains of sand in that giant hour glass it is so, as charged. But at the moment circumstance hadn't decided "The Future Me". If I told you, you would probably be surprised but this is not one of those outcome stories. (but it could have happened) Maybe a Spy? or maybe a Teacher? There you know. Satisfied! As Larry would caw, it doesn't matter you will always be Yes Yes the son of an Inn Keeper. And we will all reluctantly accept our Fate. Except Larry. Who will become rich and pay Fate to stay away.

But like most, probably all, college students, my days were filled with book nonsense. And beer. And wonderings. 'What to do? Who to be? A puppet looking for his strings and hoping his nose isn't noticeably too long.

My soul is built of stones and corridors. Larry's soul is pure Kansas prairie. Kansas is a vast flat nothing. It is not even flat. Topographically, Kansas is a wadded Kleenex of rumpled undulating hills covered with withered wheat. Cursed. Too many cows. Too much wheat. Too always windy. Excluding those funnel clouds dancing across the horizon pulling reluctant barns apart. Locusts. Grasshoppers.

Frogs. Kansas is surrounded by stuff like itself. Larry thought he could escape himself. Wrong! If you want to breathe @ Colorado. If you want to scream @ Oklahoma. If you want to look smart @ Nebraska. If you want to fiddle @ Missouri. But if you stay put and punch holes in the ground, they will fill with oil and you will become very rich indeed.

Like Larry Lanigan.

Even though Larry was just crossing fifty and I could see 25 just ahead. None the less, Larry was one of my mentors. We were angry at the same things. Although for very different reasons. Larry was black sticky guck rich. The gawkers said that when they dug his grave they will surely strike a gusher, He not only owned the stuff shirt hotel, but owned Kanigan Motors his Cadillac dealership in Eldorado Kansas. Noon, and the once poor cattle ranchers would saddle up in their Cadillacs and roam about town as if the GM Chariot was a show dog on a leash. The chrome glitter was so spectacular, it was like someone had lifted the lid of a jewelry box in a solar eclipse.

No more free dinners at The Petroleum Club. No more thick slabs of rich tender beef. Cooked rare, of course. And on the bottom of the china plate a puddle of blood and juice. In early December, Mom phoned that Mr. Lanigan had taken a hunting rifle, walked over to the used car hut, and blew his face off of his neck. The used Cadillacs looked at each other, blinked their head lights, and fell back fast asleep. Why? No one could understand why? But I knew. Larry Lanigan was broke. And there isn't enough chrome in this whole world to hide the dark. Or at least disguise it. I should never have come home. It would be a very different Christmas for this chastened Inn Keeper. It is a sin to celebrate a myth you no longer believe. Or it should be.

We weren't home five minutes when the phone rang. The Motel! …

The Manager had fallen in a stairwell. Nothing well about it. I was suddenly the son of an Inn Keeper. I swear God cursed my father for his hubris in building an authentic Victorian Inn in the middle of a Kansas scrub land. He found this Inn illustration in a copy of "Great Expectations" and fell in love with it, The family wasn't that enthusiastic. We weren't enthusiastic at all. More dumbfounded than enthusiastic.

Need I even mention the Christmas decorations that sit out front of the office. The English carriage was purchased from the Circus. The carriage axel cracked from the combined weight of the FAT lady and the world's STRONGEST MAN!. They were punished by being forced to march behind the elephants In the "Hospitality Gazette", Dad saw an advertisement for a complete life-size set of the Nativity Scene Stable. Three sheep. Three shepherds. Three kings. Three camels. A Mary. A Joseph. And finally a Baby Jesus in a Manger. Half-price from a company in Hong Kong. The figures were all life-size, they also had Chinese faces.

My Brother painted a moustache on Baby Jesus and I dressed one of the shepherds to look like an Inn Keeper. And why not. Dad didn't say anything. I think he appreciated the cooperation. The Nativity Scene became a family heirloom.

Down the East Borough Road, I turned from cracked asphalt of broken government promises to the slick cement of Interstate Highway 54. A Miracle! A full parking lot and a dangling NO VACANCY. Unbelievable! Christmas Eve being the slowest day of the year. Definitely, a Miracle! The Shepherd Clan who had booked most of the rooms were celebrating a family reunion. And as I pulled in, you could hear them singing Christmas Carols in the quadrangle.

The English Village Motor Lodge squats between King Van Lines (we deliver everywhere) and Bethlehem Steel Mid-West Regional Office, now a Kansas State Revenue Branch. Floating towards the Motor Lodge end was an intense white light. Could it be? Could a new Redeemer be born tonight? We would be famous. Just because it was the light of a B-52 landing at the Lindberg Air Force Base doesn't mean a Redeemer isn't still possible. A whirl of memories explodes. It's an omen all right, Standing there a young man, a lone, filling his suitcases with his life. So when I grow old, if that is the registry of my days, will I be strong enough smart enough to understand what happened. Will I remember them in the night of the almost redeemer. One thing I know for sure.

I will be standing somewhere alone. Wondering what all these people are doing at the English Village Motor lodge.

"*Mrs. Henrietta Fitzpatrick speaking to you*" (curtsy and bow required) Now Henry and Henrietta Fitzpatrick are on their way from San Diego to Fort Myers Beach and needed a room – no – accommodation. They must view the room before they register. Mrs. Fitzpatrick left Henry at the wheel and opened the back door of their Rolls Royce. Mrs. Fitzpatrick retrieves a cage with a parrot inside, yakking and yakking with an English accent – of course… I open the door quickly. I had never sold a room to a yakking parrot. FROGS!

FROGS. Hundreds and hundreds of jumping frogs flew across the room. Everyone was screaming. No matter how much charm you can exude you cannot beat some two hundred crazed frogs. Try catching them. I am sure there are some still around, A flood control project behind the motel was in the bulldozer stage disrupting the frogs nests. The maid had forgotten to close the bathroom window.

FROGS! A PLAGUE OF FROGS! Larry would have loved each and everywhere one of them. Please sing (You will never be alone with two hundred frogs in your room. How could I have forgotten the frogs. For surely God cursed my father for his hubris in building an authentic Victorian Inn between nowhere and nothing. Whipped whirling tumbleweeds rushing anywhere but here or even next to there. The wind had long ago blown all the trees to Colorado.

It was now almost three o'clock and no Holy Family had appeared. I had almost lost faith in myth when a rattling screeching Ford Pickup truck died in a billowing cloud of smoke. Right on cue, the Holy Family appeared. Mr. Joseph Jesus Morales's wife "Mary" was giving birth to their first child. Unfortunately, like the biblical story, I had no empty room. But I forgot about the storage room where there was a daybed for the staff. An hour later the baby was born. The Holy Family was so excited; I was utterly disappointed.

HAIL MARY FULL OF GRACE

Encore

Fitting, to say the least, that we leave each other with my own moment of truth. It happened in a Doctor's office in Madrid. I was sick with hepatitis. Real sick. The Doctor spoke very rapid Spanish whereas, I spoke very slow Spanish. "You have six months to live." Well, that was casual. I wanted a beer. That is all I could think about my mortality. And I hate beer. I have always hated beer. And if I should end up in hell, it would be the circle of an eternal Octoberfest. The doctor saw I was some what upset. "No, no, no, no! You cannot drink for six months." In the Madrid accent, 'V' and 'B' sounds are very similar: 'vivir' to live and 'beber' to drink. I am doomed to be funny.

But the Madrilanos told me not to believe doctors (what do they know). To get better, you must drink Spanish wine. It is of the earth. So, I didn't get any better. And finally had to leave Spain. Leave my soul behind in the Plaza Mayor. And have never returned to find it. I am soul less. And maybe that's why over the years I could understand so many people's burdens.

Every time I hear a lone motorcycle fading in the distance, I think of Logan and wonder what happened to his life. But I am really thinking of the lives of all the students I have ever taught, having them for just a little while, and as an old teacher, one who is dying, I realize I have come to understand the spectacle of life. And yet, still, I do not know what it all means. My words are words spoken in the dark.

Backword

British Columbia is rampant with many mountains and many lakes. They're everywhere. Therefore, it is unusual, if not downright mythological, that you would find a particular mountain, a certain lake, that – for you – would become a very special place, a refuge really, where you can be who you really are. Very special places are not easy to find and even more difficult to explain. Difficult to explain because there is magic involved. And when there is magic involved, there is a trick involved. So, you can easily be tricked into playing the fool. Seeing what really isn't there.

I tried in the stories you have read to capture for you the magic of this very special place that a map labels 'The Kootenays'. I didn't succeed, but I did try. You should know that. I did try.

The Kootenay Indians. The People of the South Wind. They were first to sense the magic. That's why they buried their dead here. A place where their kind could rest for as long as the land lasted green. Nothing *is* forever. Nothing **IS** forever.

My very special place is where dreams come to die. Most move on – leaving their dreams behind them. But… a few would stay, having found something inexplicable in its forests, mountain meadows, and waterfalls. Something to replace their lost dreams. Nothing lasts very long in the Kootenays, like the chill inside an August rainbow. The prospectors' gold and silver dreams barely lasted at all inside cold hard mountain rock. In this lush fertile terrain, the Indians would too often starve to death. And they did.

Elephant Mountain (it resembles a sleeping mammoth – though a neighbour firmly believes it resembles an alligator) rules this very special place. It was born inside a volcano some two hundred and fifty million years ago, near where the Hawaiian Islands are today. And then it walked its way, slowly, very slowly, to rest here in the Kootenays. Where it is dying. Worn away by rain and wind and heat and cold. Every spring when the creeks gush with their brown water, Elephant Mountain bleeds. Elephant Mountain knows death. It lives with it every moment that it is alive. A reminder. A reminder to enjoy inside your pain what you have while you have it.

The first people may have been born of the South Wind, but the first people knew they would eventually enter what they knew was the valley of lost souls. Lost their way. Lost their selves. Those loses were for the white others who came with all their paraphernalia. The first people would wander no more. Buried now in the soil of this valley – their true and only home. Lost to life, then welcomed through the portals of time. But… for all the peoples who left their invisible footprints on this sacred soil, there is another reality to consider. Once alive nothing is ever truly lost. The earth is a giant book of memories in shelf after shelf of rock. Loss is really change. And you must change to be alive. You can't be eighteen forever. Why the young cannot conceive the wrinkles and flab and calm satisfaction of the elderly.

Like Elephant Mountain… for example… The mountain that appears so massive is being washed away grain by grain into the Pacific Ocean, where its grains will eventually become another mountain. If the sun, permits.

Elephant Mountain is very wise. Wise because… Because it understands the times inside a 'Life', since it has lived through so many times, so many lives. Same melody, different lyrics. And of course, it not only understands the rigors of living, but also the reality everything must die. How quickly life begins in the womb and ends in some tomb. Despair? The mountain? Never! Because it has learned in all its travels that all those large and little lives will always be alive somewhere, somehow, in something. As long as the sun permits. But there will always be another sun shining on someone like us. There always will be some cantankerous bacteria slouching around some place.

So, don't be sad, or afraid about life. Live life to the fullest as the fates allow.

Elephant Mountain rules this particular narrow valley with its lake, so placid and serene. The mountain has a rock outcropping that looks like a giant eye. The eye is shut. The mountain is sleeping. It doesn't have to see you. It knows you are there because the mountain knows your dreams.

For the families who stayed behind, I taught their children, college kids, for some thirty-eight years. YES! You read it right. Children! Kids! The sooner a college instructor learns that college students are still children the sooner the instructor appreciates their dilemma. And his own. These old kids hold onto their innocence with a stubborn tenacity. Even as they feel their innocence is slipping from their grasp. I watched their agony for some thirty-eight years. These nearly people want to have fun and duly make fun of everything around them because everything around them has hidden tiny little definitions.

They are being defined and they know it. And resent it. To stop the defining, they lash out in wild compulsive acts. If you live in a drug world, or drink, drink, drink, you stop the defining. You are in your head, anyway, still a kid. You are free! When you know, you are not supposed to be free! Your head and body are speaking to you. "Accept your definition and you will be at peace with yourself. Otherwise Rancour."

A teacher is walking his dog along a highway. A young lady jogging by, stops. "I was a student of yours." She is not even winded. "Last week, I found some essays I wrote for your class." She is sweating – slightly. "I want to apologise. How could I have been so naïve? How could you not burst out laughing?"

She continued jogging through her life. I continued walking my dog through mine.

I am standing in the hallway in front of my office talking to some students. The president of the college walks by, stops. "Why are there always students hanging around your office?" "Because they are looking for solace."

About the Author

There are few things in this world that pride themselves on being old. One being Potomac University (1789) in Washington D.C. And pride galore over its 1880 Manning Hall.

Red fire brick and mismatched windows made the sagging 1789 hulk so pathetic that it wasn't worth the1812 British torch. Anyway, the colonists deserved it. But Manning Hall would have lit a spectacular bonfire. Made of hefty gray stones from Jacob's Ferry, copper roof tiles, marble floors, not one but three towers, and a portico for horse drawn carriages. Manning Hall out parliament the British Parliament.

Manning Hall was the mad vision of Potomac University's Eighth Regent: Monsignor Thomas Vincent Manning S. J. Known clandestinely as 'The Hound!' Monsignor knew everyone's sins (who they should not be sleeping with) and (where they kept their wallet and tax machinations). Seven years it required to build Manning Hall. The Monsignor always running out of cash. And the Monsignor would joke: "To the confessional I go" and "Bless the church going dunces in their faith." Seven long turbulent years of cajoling, conniving, bickering, and tantrums.

On the afternoon of the dedication of Manning Hall, the guests, all patrons, sat reverently in the golden glow of donation plaques that still line the corridors of Manning Hall. Monsignor Thomas Vincent Manning S. J. sat erect on the dais in an ornate Henry the Eighth throne stuffed full of red velvet pillows. Liver cancer stripped him of his wealth of fat. His cassock hid his chartreuse tainted flesh. Monsignor Manning S. J. did not utter a single word during the celebration. Neither did the old Jesuit tip over – not even once. Although he tilted a lot. Probably in prayer thought the congregation. Monsignor Thomas Vincent Manning S.J., Eighth Regent of Potomac University, had gone utterly mad.

A short cut through the always dank basement of Manning Hall got me to the cafeteria before the mash potatoes lumped into clots. I would always rush a hustle down the Manning basement hallway because, because I feared meeting the apparition of Monsignor Manning S.J. Supposedly, Monsignor Manning lived somewhere in the environs of Manning Hall. His statue is frightening enough! The statue is sitting out front of the Manning Hall portico. The Monsignor is not sitting on a horse like every other statue in Washington but is sitting in an ornate metal throne. The statue deemed the old S.J. did not own a twit of humour. Not even when his face was painted orange one Halloween night. Not even when buckets and buckets of turpentine were used to scrub his visage. Not even when the Monsignor still glowed an ever so delicate pink, especially in the shafts of autumn sunlight. And finally, not even when the university had to eventually buy him a new head.

Many a student, often drunk, usually drunk, have encountered the phantom of Monsignor Manning S.J. who would pass them in the basement hallway wishing them a good night. By name. That did it. By their god given Christian Name'. That usually stopped them from binge drinking – (at least for a weekend or two). Higher education can only be endured sober for five days a week.

Heavy, it was, definitely heavy, and wooden, and arched, with a large iron door handle. The bronze letters read: "ARCHIVES." The sign looked dusty. It was dusty. Obviously, Potomac University forgot it had an 'Archives'. I thought the door was, definitely, a portal to an ancient kingdom with definitely a draw bridge. And a princess with blonde locks locked in a stone tower. I wasn't dating at the moment. Many moments. Too many moments.

One evening, not very hungry, I decided to see if the door would open. Definitely, a secret passage to Hell. Let the mash potatoes clump into gulping lumps.

Inside there was only one light, from an iron lamp, probably rusted, although it was too dark to really tell. The probably rusted lamp sat on a heavy wooden desk. Hunched over what looked like an ornate Medieval tome was a Jesuit. Father Smyrna S.J. Ph.D. (twice over). As the years became decades, he had become heavy and wooden like everything else in the Archives. Father Smyrna was very old, old enough to have transcribed the medieval tome he was reading.

Father Smyrna was startled, startled enough by the scrape of the heavy wooden arched door that his thick reading glasses nearly slid off his long nose. His long nose had a definite tiny bump at the very end. It prevented startled reading glasses from sliding off. I noticed one other thing. What he wore on his gnarled arthritic fingers. Rings. Ornate rings. Three of them. Very expensive!

Because they were large and old. I guess the vow of poverty stops at the Archives heavy wooden arched door.

Father Smyrna mentioned that I had taken a wrong turn to reach the cafeteria. And Monsignor Manning did not room in the Archives. Right then and there, I decided my soul needed to know this man. Anyway, I had procrastinated in choosing a topic for an English paper. Surely there was something to plagiarise here in the Archives.

I asked what he was reading. Had been reading. Exorcism. Twelfth century chants to tame the demon. Father Smyrna, it seems was a scholar of the occult. Father Smyrna had penned two texts on modern Satanic possessions. This kind and gentle man believed there is evil in this world (Manning Hall was built on it) but doesn't believe devils are hiding in the shadows to leap out and snatch your innocence.

When the brain doesn't work right, it creates the madness that becomes Lucifer. The insane are formidable and he no longer had the strength to endure a prolonged battle with human darkness. There is no evil outside the human brain.

Father Smyrna S.J. smiled wickedly. "Searching for an essay topic, are yee?" "Yes, definitely." I didn't want him to know I am the type of person who opens doors indiscriminately. "Few students stumble in here, but when they do, I advise the same book. A book by Lewis Carroll. 'The Hunting of the Snark' (An Agony in 8 Fits). You know he was mad. Lewis Carroll. Fixated on his Alice like he was. His stories tormented her as they tormented this very unhappy mathematician. Don't you think it is hilarious – certainly ironic that this despairing man should end posthumously as a writer of children's literature. He was truly the ''Wizard of the Absurd'. With each book, the absurd becomes darker and more menacing. The absurd in the 'Hunting of the Snark' is complete with his despair. Do not be fooled by his jolly rhyme schemes."

"The map the ship's captain uses is utterly blank. The Hunt from the start is doomed. Like the Pequod. The passengers are defined by the letter 'B' (Banker, Baker, Barrister, even a Beaver)." Father Smyrna named me, also a passenger, "Blacksmith!" Why? I don't do the gym that often. Maybe because I see so much darkness in life. "There is a warning. If you do find a Snark – be wary. If a Snark is a Boojum, you will softly and swiftly vanish away. And don't forget this. All Snarks are Boojums."

Father Smyrna S.J. believed every college student should be required to read 'The Hunting of the Snark'. A college student should have no God. They just get in the way of learning. A college student should hunt his own fate. And I hope Alice never read the Snark story because the ending is just as blank as the map at the start. Nothingness. All for naught. And I hope that some time we will find The Snark and it won't be a Boojum. But until then, my story continues.

When I joined the sedate and studious monthly college magazine 'The Campus Cryer' (In the old days through the cobble stone streets of old town, a bell ringing yelping journalist would announce the news), I agreed to write a satirical column mocking a different professor each month. Yes, I AM that naive. Father Smyrna thought it was a great idea, but then he dealt daily with the damned.

The column became 'The Back Booth at Tehans'. So, I needed a pseudonym to protect my identity. Yes, I AM that naive. Wendell R. Snark was born.

Tehans was the coffee joint across from the civil war barracks that presently housed our school. The barracks! What a creaking dump. Except the furniture. Royalty sat their asses on it! The Jesuits purchased all the lounge furniture from the German luxury liner 'The Bergenville' that was trapped in New York harbour at the start of world war two. Stripped. It became a troop ship. A German U boat sunk The Bergenville off the coast of Ireland. Only the furniture survived. Heil Hitler!

Heil Wendell R. Snark who through an interview would each month mock one of the professors. 'The Campus Cryer' who had for a century whispered its essays was about to screech. No good would come of this tradition wrecker. The Snark was definitely a boojum.

But the professors loved it. To be chosen was a badge of distinction among the students. Each month the campus awaited expectantly to read what professor was trounced in The Cryer. Only one professor took umbrage. His tenured scholarship had somewhere over the rainbow became lonely alcoholism. His night course was known as an easy 'A' besides being a letter writing course. No one paid any attention. He would enter. Sit at his desk. And open the textbook. That was it. One night he fell off his chair. No one noticed for the longest time. Then, two husky students propped him back up on his chair. On my final transcript, my 'A' was suddenly switched to a 'D'. Protest? What's the point? Especially with what happened next.

Satire is suicidal. Tell that to Lewis Carroll. Satirists see fools everywhere except in themselves. The coffee served at Tehans was satirical. If you left your plastic spoon too long in its hot black liquid, the spoon would be eaten away leaving behind only the stem.

No one can remember or wants to remember who suggested the April edition of 'The Campus Cryer' be an April Fools edition. It had never happened before, or I gather after in the long-embattled history of Potomac University.

Lewis Carroll would have understood. What exactly? Why the '5' members of the editorial board including myself were snarked! The university wanted nothing less than the '5' of us to softly and swiftly vanish away…Boojumed the cabal of '5'. Why exactly? Well, the Jesuit proctor was one Father McDougal who would never agree to an April Fools edition. Father McDougal had to initial each page of 'The Campus Cryer' before us kids could publish. The Gods do favour the young. Father McDougal was a drunk. He was the only Chaplin in the history of the university who didn't have an office. He just wandered the campus hunting stray sinners. He was banned from hearing confessions, when he was found whiskey asphyxiated unconscious in a confessional. Many a student would cart their sins to him just to hear his penance which was extraordinary. His penance was to have you run around the quadrangle ten times – naked. If you sang Ave Maria while running, you were obligated to only five circuits and allowed to wear a jock strap. I guess the good cleric hadn't heard of 5 Hail Marys, 5 Our Fathers, and 5 Glory Bes.

Father McDougal S.J. never read any of the pages. So, The April Fools edition was interspersed with a fake edition. Father McDougal initials 'approved' on all the pages. Father McDougal is now a Chaplin of a small adobe church on a Navaho reservation in New Mexico.

FURIOUS! Fury. Fury. Fury upon us! The administration expelled all '5' of us. We denigrated the school. The Cuban Embassy used 'The Campus Cryer' to besmirch the holiness of the church. How do you explain to a mom-and-pop planning on attending graduation that you won't be wearing a cap and gown? Prison garb would be more appropriate. Or… running around the quadrangle ten times naked. Especially embarrassing after pumping up yourself with receiving honors in your oral boards. Explain? How question mark. You don't – You just don't. I can see now how impolite to count all the boxes of booze that were delivered every other Thursday morning to the rear door of the Jesuit apartments (The barracks). How impolite it was to report that the pink severed head of Monsignor Thomas Vincent Manning S.J. could be found in the archives. Naturally. And it was paraded around the Faculty Lounge full of Cuban Rum on

'Founders Day'. How impolite it was to pan the Bible as a soap opera for religious dunderheads. Since the pages had all been approved, The university lawyers concluded the institution would be sued and probably lose. Graduate the bastards. Fury. Fury. FURY. FURY UPON US!

Mom and pop have swiftly and softly vanished away. I never told them. Never did. About the expulsion and reprieve. Some things parents should never know. Mom was suspicious when the Potomac University President, Dean, and registrar refused to shake my hand. Our hands. Snarked, the lot of us.

When I cleaned out my desk in 'The Campus Cryer' office, I found on the desk a stuffed creature. It squatted on large black cardboard feet. It was quite plump dressed in rough blue corduroy. It wore a thick red belt around its plumpness. And to top it off, a red cap jauntily askew. A sort of nose. And a kind of mouth. Probably because of the bushy eyebrows, two large black button eyes would rivet you. Printed on the card: THE SNARK FOREVER. One Wendell Roland Snark was realized.

Wendell Roland Snark went everywhere my life took me. Because of my Parkinson's that arrived in my life when I was eighty, we were forced to sell our large house and purchase a condo – not a condom. When I reached to pack Wendell, all his stuffing gushed out. So, I buried Wendell Roland Snark between some large boulders behind our house on Elephant Mountain. A fitting farewell to an old friend.

For the ladies in my life:
Marcia, Katherine, Carolyn, Marilyn, Betty,
Lisa, Summer, Cordelia, Teagan, Fran and Rachel.

A perspective:
On the Eighth Day

An old man with Parkinson's is wandering through his memories that appear at night as hallucinations – one of the terrifying systems of Parkinson's. The old man was once a College English Teacher, well, for thirty-eight years he was that "Who", but now he is eighty and feels occasionally the shadow of death in the noise of his living. His alter ego, Wendell, appeared in his life long before the English Teacher Who.

So as not to be too confusing, Wendell R. Snark is don Wilson's pseudonym. Wendell R. Snark is the brash bawdy writer whereas don Wilson is the shy somewhat reclusive English Teacher. Both are gone now. Swept with the night into that eternal sleep. He never had his words published. They sat on the high shelf in the hall closet. Until – until I found them searching for those divorce papers. I would become his sister Wendella. Here is some stuff you should know before you start a read.

On the Eighth Day is the telling/// Well, you won't be reading a History, nor a Novel, and especially not a Biography. His telling is a most unusual Memoir where don's recollection of his thirty-eight years of teaching College English in the Kootenay's is presented in twenty-six mostly untitled vignettes. Untitled so the reader has no idea if a particular vignette will be funny, or sad, or shocking, or just nostalgic.

The writing style is conversational and disjointed. His dyslexia and arthritis have worsened and his very memory is failing in befuddled confusions and then sudden clarity. Parkinson's changes absolutely everything in a person's life, so the old man's telling must be unusual and unique. Don and therefore Wendell can no longer write legibly, nor print, and is now having trouble with the letters on the computer key board. Don has weakened. All tasks are slow and tedious. Walking a torment. He is slowly being isolated from people. Night is especially dreaded. That's when nightmares, vivid dreams and hallucinations appear.

If you do read *On the Eighth Day*, I hope you will better understand the unique job of being a teacher. When you touch people, they in turn touch you. The teacher carries this burden for the rest of his days. "On The Eighth Day" is also a tribute to those folks who suffer the ravage of Parkinson's.

Unique, I guess. All names are fictions since don's memory is flawed. No dates appear, since to don it is always Wednesday afternoon.

"But one Wednesday afternoon my brother woke to a dead language. There was nothing more to say All the words have disappeared there was only emptiness and a head full of tangled memories. Years later when mom died and we garbaged her life, I found in the attic a box of don's scribblings. The last years of his life his Wendell had lost the way of words. I, his sister (Wendell Regina Snark) would stitch together his final wanderings. I thought it would be a perfect end."